WHAT IS A CAMP MEETING ANYWAY?

you have not seen a Camp Meeting, or even if you have seen
e in some part of the country it may be difficult to imagine the
luence this movement had on the young nation of the United
ates and how that tradition established itself, evolved, and grew
as many as 3000 sites around the country. Even now around
00 of these places still exist, many of them active and in very close
the original form –a strong expression of community, and the
rce of many types of settlement today. Camp meetings that are
old as 229 years exist demonstrating a continuity of organization,
nning and lean concepts that inform and teach us today.

Camp Meeting, strictly speaking, is a religious meeting, usually of
ne days' duration. A Camp Meeting Ground is a place that was
ated and evolved to support religious camp meetings, originally
revivals, but evolving into seasons of preaching, cultural and
ucational events. They became permanent, developed places to
d renewal in nature and the strong experience of community.

experience a Camp Meeting Ground is to be in a place where
out, architecture, nature and human behavior have been
ganized to create a strong sense of community that is readable
n centuries later. Camp Meetings are original source material

for understanding how
land uses as diverse as re   urts, pocket
neighborhoods, condominiums, trailer parks, home owner's
associations, land trusts and even some town centers owe their
beginnings to the Camp Meeting movement.

They are also a good resource for Lean Building concepts, containing
vernacular building ideas based on craft, efficient use of materials,
and simplicity. Invention and adaptation were part of building the
many tents, cottages, dormitories and tabernacles that are part of
any Camp Meeting. The concepts of self-build, movable buildings
and compact, human-scaled structures were all part of Camp
Meeting grounds. Importantly, this movement differed from the
Utopian experiments that sometimes paralleled it. The people who
came to Camp Meetings did not establish new, separated permanent
worlds; they were not Shakers or Oneidans, Millerites or even
Amish., The ideas and social experiments, the construction and
urban concepts of the Camp Meetings were absorbed and exchanged
with the everyday world. Since these Camp Meetings attracted
thousands of attendees, they became general exchange centers for
the developing culture, society and civilization in the new country.

COTTAGE COMMUNITIES

THE AMERICAN CAMP MEETING MOVEMENT

A Study in Lean Urbanism

Sara N. Hines

Funding for the completion of this book has been donated by the Knight Foundation as part of a grant for the Project for Lean Urbanism.

Printing and distribution by CreateSpace @Amazon.com

Acknowledgements:
Rock Springs site illustration:
Framingham Chautauqua site plan:
Library of Congress and HABS collections

Library of Congress Information:
Hines, Sara N.
Cottage Communities – The American Camp Meeting Movement, *A Study in Lean Urbanism*/ Sara N. Hines – 1st edition.

ISBN: 978-0996243711
1. Architecture, 2. Cottages, 3. Urban Design, 4. Lean Urbanism, 5. American Religious History, 6. Community, 7. Site planning, 8. Land trusts, 9. Planning, 10. Small houses, 11. Tiny houses.

Hines Art Press – Ashland, Massachusetts
ISBN-13: 978-0996243711
ISBN-10: 0996243712

ACKNOWLEDGEMENTS

No effort like this happens without a good deal of encouragement and help. I want to thank Ellen Weiss who wrote *City in the Woods* on Camp Meetings and Wesleyan Grove first of all. Her book and Kenneth Brown's *Holy Ground, Too* set my feet on a path that has taken 7 years so far, and there are more miles to travel, more Camp Grounds to be visited.

Thank goodness for my oldest friend Barcy Fox who willingly proofed all the writing and for Joanne Mills who proofread the final draft on a hot July day.

Deepest appreciation to Andres Duany, who knew Neshoba County Fair Grounds years ago, Tom Low who wanted me to speak on it, as did the people at Monteagle Assembly, everybody at DPZ for their encouragement and finding the Lean seam in it all. Thank you Knight Foundation for grant money to get to the finish line.

Many more have allowed usage of materials, emailed, and talked. I especially want to thank the people in the Campgrounds who occasionally offered me a glass of water or a chance to see the interior of cottages and tents. The tremendous experience of being part of these communities, at least as a visitor, has been a gift.

****

THE KOAN OF SACRED PLACES -WHAT TO DO WITH DRAGONFLY COTTAGE?

Sometimes the nature of a building or a place doesn't fit the usual understanding of orderly places. What attracts us is something we like has nothing to do with orderliness, tidiness, or conformance to rules. Sometimes it is the evidence of time and use that connects us to our own past, the record of ideas, experiences, other ways of being in the world that we abandoned or that led us elsewhere.

When I first saw the Dragonfly Cove cottage, I was struck by the abstract relationship of forms, heavily moss-covered roof, colors from old paint jobs weathering, even the shadows of other, earlier construction. I could not imagine a modern-day life there, but at the same time, I yearned for the simple peace of such a haven. At one time the cottage was for sale and I, an architect, seriously considered buying it. The wooden interior, except for the kitchen, had never been painted. The upstairs had one bedroom that contained a double bed and bedside table. It had a small space at the top of the narrow stairs that held a writing desk and nothing more. One window only. The porch needed re-screening to keep out the mosquitoes, and unfortunately, the dragonflies as well. There was room for a couple of chairs and a sofa inside, but the kitchen had room for a table and chairs. Four small glass panes were etched with dragonfly images.

I thought about what I would do with it if I owned it. Would I paint it? Would I fix the gap beneath the door, patch, re-roof--*improve* it? Architects don't create "painterly" spaces, let things sag, improvise. That softness that holds us in front of such a place seems impossible to build new. They are free-verse, poetry, a sketch 150 years old. I realized that I led a life that required putting things in order, fixing them up, returning them to a state of newness. I realized that applying a life-long commitment to preservation might at the same time destroy the very essence of what was expressed here. I also know that if some level of preservation is not applied to these places, they will soon be gone. They are old, survivors, built with simplicity, yet fragile. We no longer pursue the lives that caused these places to be built; our continued use of them is a shadow of the power they originally had on people who came here for retreat, renewal, communion with nature and our fellows. It is a continuing dilemma: preservation and continuity, and the need to carry living ideas forward.

CONTENTS

PROLOGUE

I am walking around the old Camp Meeting site in Framingham, Massachusetts. I had heard that there was originally a replica Parthenon at the center of it, and some pieces of the stone ruins are supposed to be found at the top of the hill where it was flattened to build the structure. There was also a rail station devoted to the Camp, and they deflected the flow of the Sudbury River to create large swimming areas; the geared gates for this are still visible in the weeds on the path at the end of a block. There is a street named Chautauqua here, but there are only a handful of small cottages that could in anyway be considered Camp Meeting type cottages.

The area was given over by the town long ago for affordable housing with devastating results. While I walk, looking at old cottages, long since hacked up (one has been condemned due to an illegal renovation), a car drives by the central square--a bit too fast. Suddenly, a number of guys out working on a truck rush out into the street and yell for the guy to slow down. They know they live in a community, instinctively, even with little left of the original Camp other than narrow streets and a few closely spaced small cottages. The character of the place still tells them it has rules and anyone who comes in there will be noticed and cautioned to behave better. Some things, maybe the most important ones, don't change.

What has become apparent in studying the era that includes Camp Meetings is that the mindset of the 18th century American, the beliefs and concerns of those people who originated the Camp Meeting movement, was vastly different from the beliefs of the later 19th century and certainly of today. What is striking, then, is that the power of these places to attract attention, usage and fascination continues.

I believe this is due to the powerful sense of community formed first by the religious experience that they were created to contain, then by the cultural exchange in the new country of the United States --a society that was forming around the new ideas born of the Revolution. The strong bonding that occurred transcended decay and destruction The underlying desire to experience human community remains strong, and the success of these places creating it keeps these places alive.

It is significant that differences in camps, differences of religions, or even lack of religion, as in Neshoba County, MS, Fairgrounds, still allow for cohesive community. This is due to the complex pattern of planning, design, spatial complexities, and human scale, such that, even with loss of cottages, degradation of the character of the buildings, changes in governing structure or operating rules, the organizing urbanism continues to convey the message that *This* is a *Community*.

This book attempts to discover how that happens; what secrets can be learned about organizing spaces, human scale, proximity, design, and subtle tricks of planning that sustain the experience.

When the exploration of Lean Urbanism began in 2013, the Camp Meetings seemed a logical place to look for insights about historically lean practices. Camp Meetings were the precursor of such concepts as land trusts, compact and affordable housing,

community based design and many more lean ideas.

Economy of structure, integrating form with structure and ornament were certainly part of it. The planning concepts, the sizes and shapes of the outdoor spaces were another. The clear example of livable places that could be built by individuals in a way that was in no part a "shanty town" was important. The invention of detail that arose using simple parts with care and imagination, a love of geometry and craft aligns well with the concept of a lean urbanism that wants to bring back those skills. The Camp Meetings are about lean, innovative thinking and invention. The archetypal lessons of the Camp Meeting have meaning for today and for finding a new direction toward lean urbanism.

The period from 1786 to the end of the 19th century has the strongest examples of building creating community. After that, a great deal of wealth poured into campgrounds, particularly those in desirable vacation locations. The cottages, once simple, became large and costly as more people took to the lifestyle. The roadway patterns expanded with the structure sizes to support this wealth. Chautauqua, NY, is a highly successful place today; the old sections are excellent, but the expansion areas resemble the average American suburb with large ranch houses and multi-car garage doors replacing the old series of porches, rather than the close, walkable community that is so striking elsewhere. Chautauqua's older areas have strong examples of structures that would be hard to replicate today: a five story wooden hotel, dense walkable neighborhoods with dramatic pavilions and large-scale Victorian houses. But that lean, simple feel is lost on venturing into the modern areas.

Over time, some campgrounds have become condominiums and all design control has been lost. Others have become summer camps and no longer represent a community for all ages. Some have failed and been abandoned. The best examples of lean community, lean architecture, and lean urban design are still found in the early camps where the essential concepts were invented and worked out in those beginning years. The pressures for change have been many since then. Those communities that have found ways to maintain the essential elements, the patterns of community and design continue to be successful, while others have been lost entirely or have blended into the chaos of ordinary American development since WWII. A movement that had over 3000 camp meetings at its height has only 1000 remaining, but they still inform and amaze us.

Top, left to right:
Remaining Cottages in Framingham
Chautauqua; Original cottage, Framingham,
compromised by poor renovations.

Middle: Overscaled addition in Laconia,
NH Campground; large, upscale Victorian in
New York Campground;

Right: A well preserved, fine-grained Camp-
ground street, Asbury Grove, Hamilton,
MA.

CHAPTER 1--HISTORY OF THE CAMP MEETING MOVEMENT

Though it is not the intent of this book to provide an in depth religious history of the period, it is essential to have some grounding in what ideas powered this movement.

A recitation of dates and events does not begin to offer a satisfactory understanding of how the mindset and the ideas of Camp Meeting were born and why the movement took off at the end of the 18th century and lasted in many areas to the present time. That this movement parallels the origins of the United States is not a coincidence.

THE ORIGINS

Protestantism was the predominant religious orientation of the colonies and of the new nation. But Protestant sects in Europe and the Americas were rapidly changing. From the beginnings of The Great Immigration of the 17th century, the Puritan immigrants brought with them a concept that each congregation had complete ability to understand and decide all theological matters, without recourse to higher authorities for creed or control. This organization worked well enough for the original 17th century immigrants. They had been united by shared hardship and conflict, but succeeding generations lost that urgency to conform. The lure of secular wealth as the colonials succeeded weakened the congregations.

There were early 18th century attempts to reinvigorate the Puritan Church via revivals, and that experience may have influenced the later emergence of revival preaching in other Protestant sects. The Puritans eventually split into Unitarians and Congregationalists in the 19th century and did not become involved with camp meeting style revivalism. That became the province of the newer sects who were attracted to the emotional extremes and spiritual excesses that were widespread at the time. These experiences were outside of intellectualism and possibly examples of kundalini type energy experiences affecting hundreds at a time.

Methodism started in 1739 in England by John Wesley-- less than 50 years after the witch trials in New England marked both the rigidity of the Puritans and the belief in the supernatural. Methodism was a new idea getting much of its energy from the Great Awakening of the 18th century. Preaching styles for the new sect were based on intense attempts to win new converts through loud exhortation and concerns about the soul of the individual.

Methodists, Presbyterians and Baptists debated religious tenets and Ministers often changed religions. People were often converted to one religion, then another. The ideas that would fix the progress of the next age of the society were being hammered out. It is notable that Brigham Young, who succeeded Joseph Smith as leader of the Church of Latter Saints (Mormon) had been a Methodist circuit rider before his conversion.

The 18th Century is also known as the Age of Enlightenment because of the emergence of modern concepts about human rights, equality and the ability for people to remake the rules for society and their own lives. The basis for creating the United States as the first democracy in modern times derived from this new sense of power. These political ideas were conceived in a secular discourse influenced by the evolving religious ideas.

The primary political event of this era was the American Revolution. The new Americans threw out the strongest political and military force on the planet at the time–the British Empire, and created the first modern era democracy. That same vitality that allowed them to redraw the very concept of modern government extended to re-writing the concepts of God and religion. Indeed, the new country of the Western Hemisphere was often seen as a kind of new Eden–a place to perfect government, religion, and human life.

THE FIRST MEETINGS

As suggested, the concept of revival had been used by the Puritans; but Presbyterians, Baptists and Methodists were the chief initiators in the early establishment of camp meeting style Revivalism. Methodists quickly became the dominant group spreading the movement. John Wesley had sent Bishop Francis Asbury to the Colonies to spread Methodism, and he brought the idea of circuit riding preachers and aggressive preaching techniques to bring about dramatic conversions of souls. During the American Revolution, Asbury was considered a British sympathizer; his work on spreading the word of Methodism had to be suspended till 1786 when the Revolutionary War ended and the Constitution for the new country was being created.

The exact time and place of the first organized camp meeting is open to debate. Revival style preaching had been practiced from New York to the frontier, usually at small churches, even barns, as the popularity spread and attendance grew. Events spontaneously went on for days and people stayed over on the grounds. Ultimately such events overwhelmed local churches and village accommodations and meetings were moved into fields or "groves".

Claims are made for the first organized meetings being on the Kentucky frontier, in North or South Carolina, in 1799, 1794, and 1786 respectively. In Kentucky, two brothers, one a Methodist and one a Presbyterian minister, organized and preached at a meeting that might have had the first overnight campers. Known as Cane Ridge, it was held about 20 miles east of Lexington, Kentucky in 1801, and was said to have drawn as many as 20,000 people at a time when the population of the Lexington, the capitol, was only 1800. People came on foot, by wagon, horse, or ox cart and stayed for more than a week. As the experiences gained popularity, often teams of preachers –as many as 30--of various sects, served to keep the preaching going continuously -- for days.

The popularity of these dramatic meetings spread–this kind of oup event had not been experienced before. Conversions often ame with people falling into religious ecstasies, speaking in ngues, leaping, shouting or falling into profound altered states. ome meetings spontaneously lasted for weeks. It was estimated at by 1860, a million people had experienced a camp meeting.

he Methodist circuit riding preachers became involved with evising layout standards and rules for these encampments, hich initially had the spontaneity of a Woodstock (1969) by omparison. There was a steady transition from local churches to cal land that could be acquired and camp meetings would be eld as often as every quarter. Local elders were given authority to nd and organize the sites.

rom the start, people clustered around a central speaker, usually et up on a raised platform, often referred to as a brush arbor or abernacle, and set up their tents or wagons at the perimeter. At ight the events continued with pine knot torches, bonfires and ontinued preaching, singing, and shouting. Tents, preaching ands, and campfires were the organizing features of the first eetings.

eligious leaders looked for land with ample water, area to pasture tock animals, and topography that allowed meeting space and the bility to lay out campsites. Rules for conduct and site use grew ut of the need to have as many as 10,000 strangers function as community in short order. There was the immediate need to reate a concise sense of place to contain the preaching, the ecstatic exercises", promote communal fellowship and accentuate the sense f removal from everyday concerns to focus on the event.

he crowds that showed up usually included drunks, rowdies, nerchants and curiosity seekers as well as those interested in eligion. Elders or special police were used to control the more lisruptive elements, but that attraction was part of the mission of ransforming a rough new country without organized moral rules nto a new civilization that could settle, create cities and the new ountry.

hese kinds of meetings were also one of the few communal ways o meet and exchange ideas, find potential spouses, or make

1819 Camp Meeting, Library of Congress

business connections in an environment that was made safe by the organizing structure of a such a community.

The larger task of camp meetings was to provide a civilizing vision for the unruly and chaotic era at the end of the 18th and beginning of the 19th century. .

This early era of camp meetings predated the existence of trains and that affected the planning and layout of the camps. By 1854, a *Manual for Camp Meetings* was published by one Reverend B. Weed Gorham–but that was 60 years after the pioneering meetings had been established. Gorham merely codified what had been learned.

From the earliest times, this was a movement that was being invented and revised on the spot– a true example of generative design, something that will be discussed further in the section on Planning.

In the northeast, populations found sites closer to area towns and quickly a relationship between towns for supplies, transportation and visitors became established. Consider that people had to take a long ferry ride in 1830 to get to the Massachusetts island of Martha's Vineyard to spend many weeks at a Camp Meeting.

THE MIDDLE ERA

The strong religious revival aspect of camp meetings began to wane in the 19th century, and eventually Methodism sought to shed the more exciting behaviors of the revivalists. The intellectual debates of the abolitionists and Transcendentalists could be found in the northeast and the Civil War marked a strong change in the nature of camp meetings.

The Civil War made a dramatic change in purpose for these places. One significant Camp in New Jersey was founded a mere 3 weeks after the Battle of Gettysburg, and at a distance of about 150 miles from it. The loss of life in the country was so great that virtually everyone was in mourning and the attraction to the Camp Meetings was rooted in loss and a search for peace. The power of community to heal and teach in this period was critical.

Second in significance was the advent of the train. When people no longer came with livestock and wagons, Camps could be located near rail lines and required less acreage. Camp Meetings that were founded in this era frequently had a rail stop or even a spur rail line to the location and the link between town planning and camp ground design became more clear. In New Jersey some religious municipalities were established.

By that time the Camp Meeting form was becoming normalized, incorporating what had been learned from early camps. There were manuals dealing with all aspects of the process up to the design of tents. Tents were also becoming permanent cottages. In some areas, such as Martha's Vineyard, professionals were laying out vacation expansions to the original camp grounds. In locations that had good prospects, the new idea of Vacation insured the continuation of the Camp Meeting.

The Camp Meeting must be seen as separate from the Utopian movement that it paralleled in the 19th century–those social and religious experiments such as the Shakers, Mormons, Millerites, Oneidans, or Swedenborgians. The difference is that Camp Meetings and their proponents were well intergrated into everyday society so that there was ongoing exchange of ideas and behaviors.

LATTER TIMES· THE RISE OF CHAUTAUQUA

It was difficult to keep some of the highly developed Camp Grounds active for an entire season, which could be from April to October in the northeast, so Camp Associations began to invite other civic groups to use the grounds.

The Chautauqua movement began in 1874 in Chautauqua, N.Y. as a movement to educate Sunday School teachers and it quickly caught on as a system offering distance learning in many subjects with diplomas offered at the annual Chautauqua meetings. The concept of mass education for adults via this system gained popularity and kept the Camp Meetings going when they might have begun to falter. Many Camps featured Chautqua sessions.

By the end of the 19th century, interest in the movement, the religious aspect of Camps was far more restrained and the idea of community retreat, social interaction, and the culture of lectures and learning was the larger focus. The sense of community and renewal through retreat in nature was still a dominant theme. However the developing industrial and technical age was to offer competition for the time and interest of the population. The period from 1874 to World War I saw some expansion and some loss of Camp Meetings. At its peak, the movement had over 3000 formal Camp Meeting grounds, but following WWI and the Spanish Influenza Epidemic, interest declined. During the Great Depression, in some areas, people moved into camp meeting grounds to escape debt collectors or simply to have shelter. Camp meeting cottages were always lean and affordable, and as always the sense of community was a strong attraction. Willimantic Camp Meeting in Willimantic, CT, and others began shifting over to year round dwelling during this period and this trend has continued.

TODAY

Many Camp Meetings continue as they have for centuries. Others have transitioned to year round communities, still others have been privatized, sold off, or re-organized into various different forms of home ownership. The concept of governance and the future of these places is discussed further along.

It is extremely rare to find new cottages built to original standards as codes make it difficult to achieve this. Loss of multiple cottages by fire is a disaster because of the near impossibility to rebuild in this way. But in some areas one can find rebuilds in historically protected camp meetings, mostly in the south where "tents" as they are usually referred to there seem to evade characterization as dwellings.

It is possible to visit active Camps, whether the continuously held Rock Springs Meeting in Denver, NC, in August with thousands in attendance, or to a Spiritualist Camp Meeting in Lily Dale, NY, experience community in much the same way as it has always been. The experience is still powerful and one that seems profoundly different from modern life–more direct, more personal. We hardl have such experiences available to us these days.

The variations of the Camp Meeting form were adapted by other religious groups seeking community. The evolution of the Camp Meeting and its survival for 230 years owes that success to the complete picture of the Camp Meeting from essential design, land ownership, governance, and the people who participate, often for generations.

Camp Meetings are both simple and lean, complex and obvious. The fine understanding of human space and behavior, of lean and beautiful "tents", cottages, streets and neighborhoods resulting in deeply sensed community is source information for creating enduring settlements again today. The proof of this is the continuing ability to attract thousands to these places every year. This is the legacy of the Camp Meeting Movement.

Camp Meeting Preaching --old drawing --Library of Congress

West Branch Camp with two story tents - detail view--Library of Congress

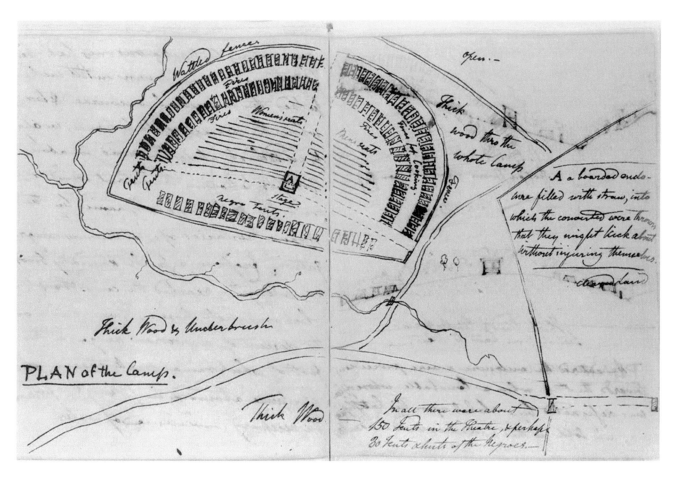

Old Camp Meeting Plan showing slave tents behind preaching stand--Library of Congress

Red Lion (PA) Camp, typical early camp showing tents -- Library of Congress

Above: Dorms at Asbury Grove Camp and a 16' wide cottage. Below: Illumination Night street, afternoon, Wesleyan Grove, Oak Bluffs, Martha's Vineyard, MA, showing luminaria set up along he street.

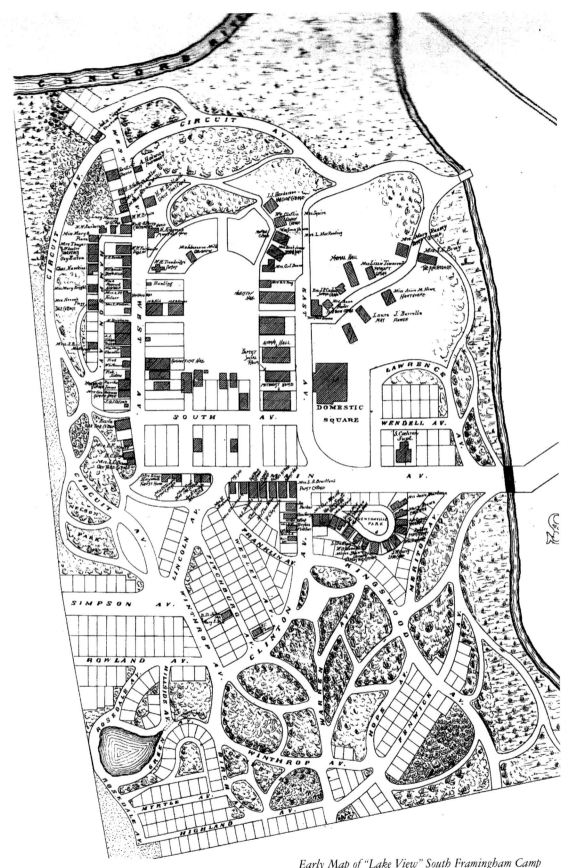

Early Map of "Lake View" South Framingham Camp
Meeting Association --Framingham Historical Society

CHAPTER 2 -- PLANNING CAMP MEETING GROUNDS

West Branch, PA, two story tents -- Library of Congress

Above: Camp Woods, Ossining, NY, founded 1804
--Library of Congress
Left: Camp Woods Gardens today, Camp Woods has become a
condominium - small interconnected spaces are visible in
the older print as well as in the current plan.

SITE PLANNING FOR CAMP MEETINGS

While religious ideas and revivalism started the movement, the creation and evolution of community sustained it throughout all the changes in society that marked the next 200+ years. That the form of these Camp Grounds could adapt to changing needs of a growing movement demonstrates the strength of the designs, which were constantly being adapted and improved. The physical layout of the space, the building designs, the planning, land use concepts, and the operational rules governing the meetings all reinforced community in ways that are palpable today when we walk into one of these places—even when that place has lost much of the original finish and purpose. Camp Meeting grounds are a testament to the simplicity and efficiency of how land can be organized into patterns that generate community and deliver that sense of place to people who come there. There is a lean essence to this kind of planning.

The earliest Camp Meetings were experiments. In that sense, they became generative in their design evolution and the earliest camp layouts reflect that. Ossining, NY, Camp Woods, founded in 1804, is a good example of one of the early layouts where the remains of this generative style are still apparent. An old print shows the nature of the early camp. It is made up of a number of sub-centers connected by pedestrian paths. It was not centralized then and remains that way today. The illustrated view is from the layout today, now that it is simply a condominium. It still shows different focus areas and a pedestrian path system completely separated from the one vehicular loop, plus two separate tabernacles, one fairly small, the other probably enfronting the original larger preaching area.

Non-negotiable basics were learned through early failures, often painfully. First, an adequate water supply was crucial; then, there had to be enough food. Running out of either meant that the meeting would end prematurely, as happened in early experiences. The grounds had to support the large numbers of people and the ideal sites were level or slightly sloped. There should be a canopy of shade, nearly complete, ease of access by local thoroughfares, and a central location within the district. A wood supply available for tents and cook fires and nighttime torches was essential.

In the earliest years, it is important to remember that nothing moved faster than the speed of a horse. There were no trains -- people came by horse, ox cart or even by walking. These are places for pedestrians, though, particularly in the northern camps when cottages had replaced canvas tents, people would bring essential furniture just for the season and that would be delivered using a few narrow carriageways. Room to pasture livestock was critical and was routinely located at the outer edges of the site. The pattern of placing vehicles at the outer edges of camps evolved from this and is still a prevalent pattern.

The impact of the train on these popular meetings changed the nature of new camp layouts. The result then was even more pedestrian dominated space, This influence can be seen in places like Pitman Grove, NJ, and in very rural camps where the access to the site was much easier by rail than by road (Camp Greene,

RI). These later patterns also began to reflect urban forms as grids or more rationalized layouts. Where early patterns suggested pathways and fine-grained response to topography and activities, later layouts suggested more professional planning.

In the early campgrounds, the idea of growth in camps required constant adaptation. The popularity of Camp Meetings grew and these places attracted crowds that were unprecedented. Learning how to respond to those numbers must have been difficult–the only precedents must have been conducting a war, and the Revolutionary War was a near memory for the early Camp Meeting visitors. Finally, the first purpose for a camp meeting was preaching for conversion or revival and the immediate layout had to support that.

The second purpose, which was the long term gift of these places, was a community of fellowship. The founders of Camp Meetings understood this; it is stated in the early Camp Meeting manuals. This part of the Camp Meeting was at least as important as the religious aspect. What they could not have known is that the community part of Camp Meetings is what would sustain them through all the dramatic historic and cultural shifts to come and what would allow these places to survive.

Early manuals on how to create Camp Meeting grounds included simple advice based on knowledge gained from the first years, but the manuals were not written until sixty years after the earliest meetings were established, so experience informed the written wisdom.

The most basic rules included:
As stated above, land: flat or slightly sloping, adequate water and

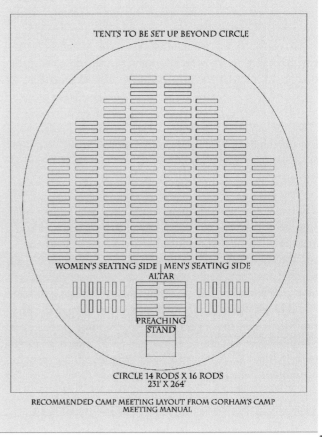

CIRCLE 14 RODS X 16 RODS
231' X 264'

RECOMMENDED CAMP MEETING LAYOUT FROM GORHAM'S CAMP MEETING MANUAL

pasturage for livestock. There were also rules about what work to do several weeks in advance: clear land, stack cut wood for tent poles and camp fires. Preparations were also made to construct tents from yardage of "factory cloth". Planning was concise and lean, presuming a certain amount of work from the attendees.

Decisons about how distances were to be laid out were based on acoustics -- how far voices carried. Besides concern about how many people would attend, attention focused on how far away one could hear a speaker, how far away to site a tent so that domestic sounds would not carry back to the crowd of people listening to the speaker.

Though level ground was preferred, in the end sites were built on all sorts of land. In Boulder, CO, the Chautauqua there is built on a steep mountain. In Tennessee, in the southern Appalachians, one finds dense woods by streams capable of flooding or on hills requiring pedestrian trestle bridges. In New England they are sited on islands requiring ocean travel. In Pennsylvania, one very large Camp was established by a river that completely wiped it out; in that case, it was never rebuilt. (West Branch, p. 16)

In these early 19th century camps the recommended site plan form was round or oval and followed very specific guidelines. They were to be 14 rods by 16 rods, with seating divided by gender and with an altar area where those who felt called by the preaching could come sit. Tent areas were situated beyond the circle. Historic photographs often show these layouts complete with board seats and the tents surrounding the area.

Ossining, NY, is the location for Camp Woods, dating from 1804, has a central area and several extensions or sub-areas rhat may have also been established by sound distance. The need to break off separate areas to offer space for more preachers, and to accommodate the short distances needed to hear speakers was a logical factor. There was no amplification other than how far a voice would carry from a preaching stand, usually designed to be about 6-1/2' above the crowd. Acoustics limited preachers, yet there could be thousands of people attending. What often happened was placing other speakers at appropriate distances. This kept the original scale small, though when tabernacles or pavilions became popular, the acoustics improved and centralized the organization. The very large covered tabernacles changed the designs again.

We also forget how quiet the background noise was in a pre-vehicle countryside. Ideally one could sit in front of one's tent and hear the preaching. This is still observable, particularly in southern camps. The large field surrounding the tabernacle became a space where more preaching could occur, or over the years, children play and people could stroll. If the numbers of visitors got larger, they would logically add new spaces rather than enlarge the first space to a scale that no longer functioned. At some of the largest early meetings there might be as many as 20-30 preachers, some at opposite ends of a field, reportedly with people running from one area to another if the level of interest increased.

The preaching style created what must have amounted to an altered state of consciousness among the thousands who attended. Attendance in such numbers alone was unheard of at the time. Keeping this experience going required some experimentation with size of space, number of speakers and frankly, containment of those attendees.

It is no mistake that the earliest encampments were closed circles or squares. Keeping out rowdies and drunks was part of the issue, though they wanted to attract the worst miscreants for conversion, too. They needed the intensity of the experience to get the desired result.

The stories of preaching all day and going into the woods and singing in loud voice all night suggests the ecstatic experiential nature of a meeting, and the physical layout had to support these events. While we have more mass events today, the equivalent would be of a rock concert, a sporting event, or perhaps a protest in a public square. The nature of the container for the space is important. It needed to create a sense of urgency and excitement to allow the transformation to happen.

The boundary for the area tended to be porous at the same time it contained the space. Perhaps a tightly closed boundary would have been too limiting or inconvenient—or even impossible to maintain. Narrow gateways, pinch points and spaces between cottages or tents are common and part of the hierarchy or shifting scale of spaces. How those spaces affected behavior is part of the sense of community. The spatial experience goes from public, to private, to intimate and from free flowing to guarded. The small aperture openings also afford views into other spaces. In square layouts, the corners are especially interesting as they mark transition points and signal a need for behavior change to match what is happening in the larger space.

One quickly observes the close distances and adjusts the level of a speaking voice. This becomes inherent. I recall never hearing a voice raised in anger or even a crying child when I walked through Rock Springs Camp Meeting in full season just a few years ago, with thousands of people sitting on porches, walking the long paths, or sitting in the tabernacle. In the back rows there was a game of touch football, on other front porches children slept in play pens or families enjoyed dinners. People greeted passersby, they chatted across the way and along the way.

By 1850, the extreme behavior of the early ecstatic meetings was shifting, some Protestant sects had split off their revivalists, and people were, instead, hotly debating moral issues such as abolition and ethical behavior.

Why was religious conversion such a compelling factor? There was chaos and lawlessness as well as a societal shift in progress. The drive for religion was part of the drive to civilize the new country. The movement from frontier and agricultural settlement to urban societies, the growth of cities and the beginning of the industrial revolution had created challenges and models that people had not experienced. Young single people were leaving their families and going to cities to find work; crime and exploitation were widespread. People were wealthier but the systems of class, law

Indian Field Camp Meeting Ground, South Carolina, established 1794, showing continuous ring and privies to the outside. --Library of Congress

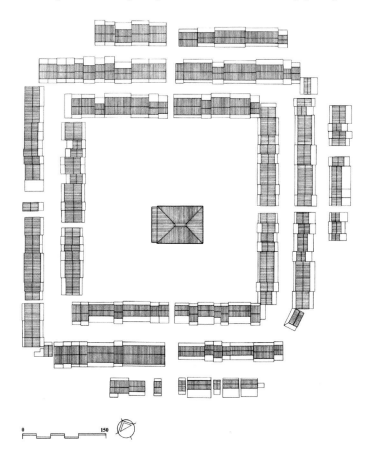

0   150

Left, top to bottom: Inner Ring at Indian Field, corner cut-through at Balls Creek Canp, NC; Cut through from rear open kitchens to inner ring at Cattle Creek Camp Meeting, established 1786.

Above: site plan of Rock Springs Camp Meeting, Denver, NC, established 1794, longest continually operating camp meeting. Note concentric rings and ccentral "arbor" or tabernacle. ... graphic courtesy of Carl Lounsbury.

Motts Creek Camp Meeting is an Afro-American camp in Catawba County, NC, Lean building here with slab-wood cottages and some use of salvaged telephone poles to structure porches. Right: hand hewn pews.

and social interaction were anything but fixed. Morality, the very sense of right and wrong, of a commonly held conscience, was only randomly settled.

Drunkeness was at a level that would eventually lead to such figures as Carrie Nation and the Women's Christian Temperance Union demanding that people "sign the pledge" (not to drink). Religion became the tool to accomplish this change.

More people were participating in Camp Meetings after the development of trains and the extension of rail lines. This era also marked the advance toward Civil War and the issue of Abolition. The sense of community in Camp Meetings supported the debate about the future of the country. As has been discussed, the era of the Civil War itself, the sense of tragedy, and the need to bring the country back together brought on the next explosion of new Camp Meetings.

The advent of trains and the lessons learned from earlier experiences acted to change new Camp Grounds being built in the north, while the rural character of the camps in the south continued. This may have marked a change in the two areas with the northern camp grounds continuing to assimilate immigrant newcomers while the southern camps strengthened the existing community. Immediately after the Civil War, Afro-American camp meetings were also created, often very close to the older white camp grounds. The layouts are similar; but the leanness of the "tents" is extreme, with structures built with salvaged materials and scrap slab wood. Pews in black camp meeting tabernacles are simple and hand hewn.

The impact of growing cities and towns on the northeastern camps can be seen particularly in New Jersey where Camp Meetings had been chartered by the state as religious municipalities, an arrangement that would last until 1979 when a religious separation was forced. These urban camps were dramatic experiments at planning complete communities or towns.

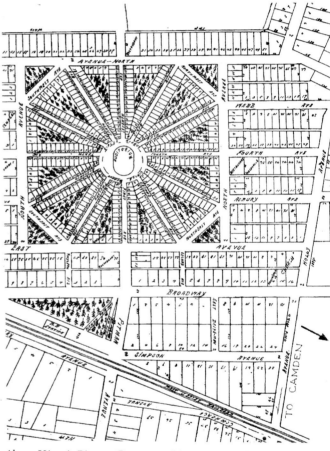

Above: Historic Pitman Grove map, Pitman, NJ--Library of Congress, The twelve paths of the Apostles shown. After "religious municipality" ruling, lots were sold off and the Tax Map to the right shows the result.

Pitman pathways, at convergence above, below typical Pitman style cottage.

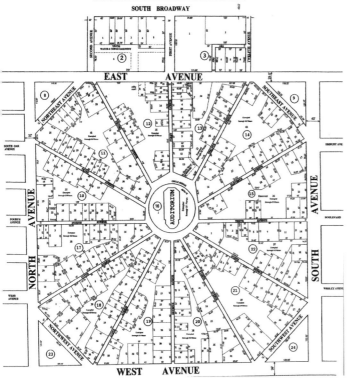

Pitman Grove was built immediately adjacent to a rail stop and became the pattern for the town of Pitman, NJ. The main street was both a normal commercial street and the supply support for the camp. One stepped off the train and walked through a gate across the street directly into the camp's system of streets and pathways or turned onto the main street.

This unusual layout of radiating narrow streets was said to have been inspired by the 12 Apostles being sent out to evangelize. The "streets" are simply pathways 5' wide or less. The density of the urban fabric spread blocks away and a cottage type that is unique to Pitman evolved. When the NJ Supreme Court ended all religious municipalities in 1979, the Camp Meeting was platted, sold off, and became part of Pitman. The result is evident in the current tax map of this area. The radiating pattern is changed by the larger lots where parcels were merged; there is no design control. It is interesting to see that the use of the "pie-wedges" that would have supported back of the house informal space have become parking areas. The small triangular parks at each corner act to form subsidiary places each with a separate name and character. The remains of this unique camp make for a tapestry of angled views and layers of community. The tabernacle has been preserved and is used for civic events, The sense of community is closely affected by the density and the pathways that support interaction, though religion is no longer the underlying connection.

Pathways meeting near the Auditorium and a view of First Street running to the Tabernacle, which is used now as a civic building for events.

Line of large Victorians along main axis to tabernacle (below left) with tents to the right of it, along side streets, behind the tabernacle and a back view of the permanent kitchen and bathroom structures. Off season, tent platforms and permanent structure wait for the April - October season. See left.

Ocean Grove, with original style tents, transitional tent-like cottages, small cottages and finally huge new Victorian Cottages.

Contrast in Ocean Grove with modern Victorian with historic cottages. Left: Permanent tent bases and support sheds housing plumbing and storage off-season, note tent supports and floors

A street in Mt. Tabor, Parsippany, NJ, another community affected by the State Supreme Court decision banning "religious municipalities".

Another major New Jersey camp ground affected by the Supreme Court ruling was Ocean Grove, in Neptune NJ. This Camp Ground encompasses one square mile of intense, fine-grained, dense urbanism and community. Ocean Grove has always been successful due to its location on the ocean with recreational attractions.

Ocean Grove is particularly interesting as it still uses 114 canvas tents as rentals that are erected each spring and taken down each fall. These tents have a history in themselves. They are constructed with a permanent deck floor and a structure at the rear that contains kitchen and bath facilities. These tents follow quite closely the traditional design with a double tent fly and scalloped edges. The tents are two rooms one in front and one to the rear. My observation is that generally the porch is the social area, with sleeping in the front tent portion while cooking and bathing are contained at the rear. The tents have just two rooms.

Ocean Grove also has a well developed commercial street and a huge wooden auditorium capable of seating 10,000. Cars were kept out of Ocean Grove on Sundays until 1979. Streets are narrow in Ocean Grove, but streets are narrow in almost all camp grounds. Streets were not designed for vehicles. That wagons came in, now and again is clear and generally a car can slowly make its way along today, even on a Sunday. Now that there is no ban on cars, the tiny streets with on-street parking are quite congested resulting in a tendency for visitors to park once and

walk. The experience is much richer on foot anyway, but notably this is one of the few campgrounds that has a vehicular traffic problem.

Ocean Grove has a fire department that is operated by the City of Neptune, but housed in fire houses owned by the Ocean Grove Camp Meeting Association that owns the land as well. The addition of fire departments is also found in Camp Meeting grounds established in the later 19th century. Lily Dale operates its own and Mt Tabor seems to cover both the Campground and surrounding areas.. Since fire is the most common threat to these places, it makes sense.

Pitman, Mt. Tabor, in Parsippany, NJ, and Ocean Grove are, more than most Camp Meeting sites, year round towns. The original camp meeting cottages were not winterized and some say that the open wood framing was an important feature that has been lost, but many buildings in these year round camp grounds are fully winterized.

A - Wesleyan Grove
B - Trinity Park
C - Forest Circle
D - Victorian Park
E - Clinton Ave
F - Commonwealth Ave

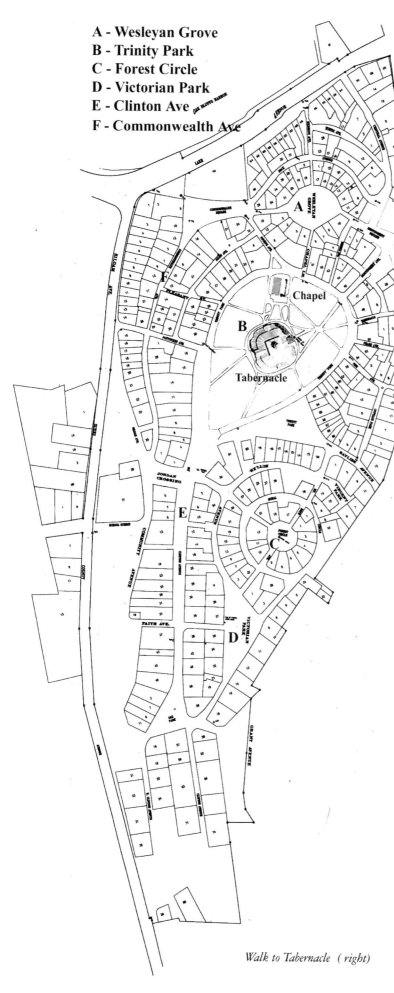

Wesleyan Grove Camp Meeting camp site plan. The earliest part of the camp is the smaller circle of Wesleyan Grove (A) with expansion to Trinity Park which holds the large tabernacle and small chapel (B). The smaller Forest Circle, about 65' in diameter (C) is another offshoot as was Victorian Park (D). Clinton Ave. (E) is an unusual pedestrian street with sidewalks along both sides and seating areas in the middle. It captures views of the large Trinity Park and acts as as a structured civic promenade. Some areas like Forest Circle act as destination places while Clinton Ave. and Victorian Park seem to best suggest strolling. Some of the narrower walkways, such as Commonwealth Ave. combine the strong sense of place along with a promenade. This relates directly to the width of the walkways that send the message of intimate space while supporting the linear strolling experience. The porches create mediating space between the public and the private space so that a comfortable experience is always available. 315 cottages remain here.

Below: Cottages in Wesleyan Circle   graphic assist, Tom Bostic

Walk to Tabernacle (right)

Forest Circle cottages

Wesleyan Grove Camp Meeting Association, in Oak Bluffs, on Martha's Vineyard, MA, is one of the most well known camp meetings, and since it spans the time from 1830 to present, it reflects many of the planning issues that the campground form has had to deal with. Early on, camp visitors arrived by boat and had to walk to the camp ground. A commercial street immediately outside the camp quickly developed to serve the needs of the visitors. The first meetings were probably contained in the small square on the north known as Wesleyan Square,

though with growing popularity, the large space at the center soon followed, supported by secondary circles, promenades and squares. About 315 cottages remain today as well as the large tabernacle, a small chapel, history museum and, of course the surrounding commercial area. Wesleyan Grove may have started the first vacation development in the country as the land beyond the immediate camp ground was soon laid out and developed with summer houses. Visiting Oak Bluffs today is an intense experience of mostly Victorian buildings of great variety and detail.

The original camp meeting site still has distinct boundaries containing the action within. Gateways could be closed to keep

Left: Commonwealth Ave. (F) a peripheral street with typical cottages .

Middle: View to a Camp Meeting Hotel at the edge of the Camp Ground --boarding houses and hotels were common.

Below: View of Clinton Ave. a pedestrian boulevard, area F on site plan. Note walks are at edge of porches for visting.

out disruptive elements.

One of the unusual characteristics of the early camps wa that buildings were moved and moved often. There is a story of a cottage owner who violated the rules of the Oak Bluffs camp meeting and was forced to move his cottage out of the camp–which he did overnight. The space has not been re-occupied but I am told the cottage is located in another part of Oak Bluffs. That these cottages were moved by teams of oxen or horses across narrow pieces of land and that they remained intact is even more surprising.

THE CONTRAST OF THE SOUTHERN CAMPS

The Southern Camps are the strongest example of contained experience. Probably because the typical southern Camp Meeting site is not in an urban context these camps needed boundaries. The plans almost resemble fortresses except for the many small porous openings connecting inner and outer rings. See Chapter 6 on Southern Camps for more.

The large circle or square with a tabernacle, often called an "arbor", is the common form. The space between the center building, generally a vast hip roof structure, and the row or circle of tents, now wood, is a critical dimension limited again, by sound transmission. One feature of all these arbor/ tabernacles was the view at the edges which is filled by the facades of the tents–a strong witnessing presence.

If one had a "tent" around the perimeter, the ideal distance allowed one to sit on the front porch and hear the preaching yet have enough distance so that domestic noise did not intrude on the activities in the center.

Two slot transitions-Wesleyan Grove above and Cattle Creek below. These control points separate formal from informal areas, public from private.

Balls Creek Camp Meeting Ground, Catawba Cty, North Carolina. Note similarity to Rock Springs Camp Meeting plan also in this chapter.

Below a corner cut-through at Balls Creek showing the view into the next row. At right the slatted openings for privacy and ventilation. The bench? A public/private accommodation.

The apron that separated a tabernacle from the first line of "tents" also supported walking from front porch to front porch as well as overflow seating from the arbor. In earliest times this area would have supported additional preachers or activities.

When one sees the larger southern camps the initial square of tents was repeated by secondary concentric rows that extended the experience offering more opportunities for socializing. Visiting Rock Springs Camp Meeting, in North Carolina, in season, it is clear that there are even more people involved in walking the back promenades than attending the meetings at the central altar.

The influence on town center design also is visible in southern towns where a similar pattern with courthouses or town halls at the center of a square and concentric sets of streets is common. Southern Camp Meeting grounds were generally found in rural areas but the concepts were readily spread by the many attendees. What was placed at the center of the community simply changed.

Walking the perimeter promenade at Balls Creek Camp Meeting Ground. Note proportions of width to height of walkway, acoustic distances, visual proximity, function of porches as transitions.

Side of block at Malaga, with just three cottages. The blue cottage is a classic cottage with front porch, living space with loft above and cooking area at the back. This basic type is found in most camps in the east.

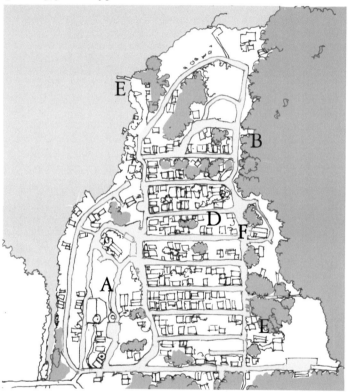

Above: Lily Dale, with activities oriented at the edges of the cottage area Below: 10' wide Asbury Grove street.

View of Malaga Block 1, typical 15' lots with 12' wide cottages

Lily Dale Assembly-left. Library and meeting auditorium, National Headquarters for the Spirtualist Church and dining facilities area A; Stores, path to Inspiration Stump, Healing Temple and other program areas plus Museum area F; housing in the center, D. Recreation areas at the lake and fields, E. A diverse rather than focused organization.

12' wide cottages on 15' wide lots yield 3' separations. Gap on right is to the left of the cottage above, and includes a door and windows.

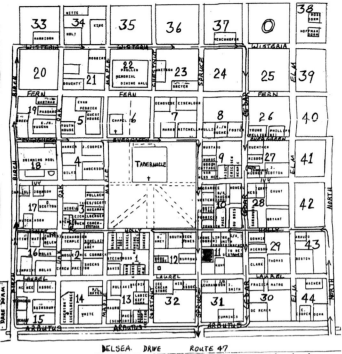

The tiny grid of Malaga Camp Meeting. Block 11 is said to be the original layout.

In some northeastern camps the central circle is empty with the preaching stand set at one end and benches filling the circle, but that dramatic center tabernacle is more common.

The exception to the center organization of these places is found in Spiritualist camps. In this religion, people practice mediumship and many are involved with offering spiritual readings to attendees. Events here are distributed around the camp and vary during the day and into the night with activities in woodland areas, perimeter temples, a library, museum, healing temples, lecture halls, and individual cottages. In season, in a place like Lily Dale, visitors are constantly walking through the streets to attend featured events in a non-centered format. Opportunities to meet up are many but dispersed.

Looking at critical dimensions, it is clear that there is no specific rule that applies to all Camps, but patterns emerge that are commonly found: residential areas are narrow but may widen to form squares, or specifically at tabernacle areas or where crowds will form. Intuitively, open spaces are contained and bounded.

The community effect is generated by physical dimensions too, and these can be studied. Asbury Grove Camp Meeting in Hamilton, MA, is a good example of the kind of space that generates community. Ten feet or less is fairly common for roadways, even when the roadways are paved. A typical width in Asbury Grove is 10' for the roadway and 18' from front of house to front of house with porches or stoops about 4' wide narrowing the roadway more, but sometimes wider when fronting squares. The street wall is about 18' high to the ridge top yielding a 1:1 ratio.

The typical cottage is 12'-4" wide with a plate height of about 12'-12'-4" with a roof pitch of 12/12 (45 degree). In the narrower

cottages that are 10' wide, the plate (point where roof rafters spring) is still about 12' but the roof pitch is usually steeper, so that proportionately it is an equilateral triangle. This relates directly to the Gorham's Camp Meeting Manual that shows a pattern that used 40 yards of fabric for a canvas tent, but it as much relates to the convenience of getting a 12' post, which was easy to get, with timbers at the top and bottom to form the frame. The cottages were typically balloon framed with about a 3' knee wall for the upper sleeping rooms. See the chapter on cottages for graphics of these tents.

In Malaga, NJ, the tiny blocks, 49 of them are about 105' long with 10'-6" roadway widths. In the center, four blocks are merged to form the green with the tabernacle located on it. The average block is supposed to have 7 - 15' wide lots but even from the beginning they altered this rigid rule. The small blocks originally had some common space in the block centers but today this is difficult to discern. Some secondary sides of blocks have only three houses on them. Distinctly the perimeter of Malaga has old barns for livestock that have been mostly converted to garages or replaced with storage sheds. This reflected the pattern of keeping horses and wagons, and later vehicles at the outside.

Neshoba County Fairgrounds, MS, tent sites are fixed, and only varies to preserve a tree. Above is backside of tents, below the social front side.

Two examples of trees growing through roofs, Pine Grove Camp. the lower house has a tree growing through the right hand small porch.

The next level of design is the size of individual campsites. In Bayside, ME, the campsite was 16' x 24', in Malaga, NJ, 15' x 30', in Neshoba County Fairgrounds, which is not religious but organized around Camp Meeting rules, the basic cabin there is to be 16' x 30' and two stories tall with 4' between cabins–and no trees should be cut. This tree rules makes for many small quirks in the plan, and relieves what might have been a tedious layout. Neshoba, like many northeast Camps has trees growing through porches.

Scrupulous retention of trees is common in most camp meetings, and it is normal to see trees integrated into porches or eaves cut back to accommodate growth as the trees and the camps aged. In some camps the remains of a dead tree, cut off, remain integrated with the cottage. In northeast Camp Grounds today, the problem can be aging trees falling, combined with ice storms and sometimes hurricanes. In some cases the damage is devastating.

Society Cottages at Plainville, CT Camp Meeting around the tabernacle. Below: site plan. Right below: green street shown at upper right on plan, connecting small cottages to circle.

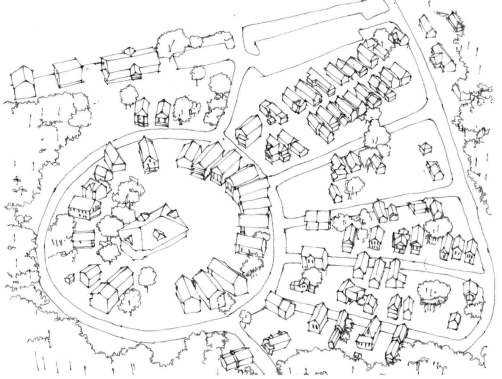

In most Camps, commercial development was limited to boarding tents and later hotels, but merchants did set up areas near these sites to sell to the large number of attendees. This early stricture against commercialization was changed by the mid 19th century. Even in a very old camp like Rock Springs (1794), there is a snack bar that sells food, cold treats and simple toys.

Notably commercial space when it is included is always outside the religiously oriented center, usually near the edges. The same is true of any hotels or dining halls, the exception being society tents. A society tent and later an association cottage was a larger

31

cottage owned by an area church for their members to use during meetings. They might hold numerous small bedrooms or common facilities. In the earliest manuals on camp meetings, these are shown as about 20' x 30' and this is a common dimension for a wooden society cottage. In old camps it is unusual to find a cottage as wide as 24'. Plainville Camp is a classic example of a campground laid out with a perfect circle of association cottages surrounding a tabernacle in a natural amphitheater area. Individual cottages are contained on narrow streets set in a grid extending off the central circle. One of these streets is actually just a green street–leading toward the center. This shows a clear division of religious or program areas from community areas.

Scale is a critical part of understanding Camp Meetings. The armature of the camp is the layout of narrow streets, scaled to human community. It is unclear if this was done with any science; it is more probable that distances were set intuitively or generatively after observing what did or did not work, and making

adjustments, or learning from past experience. This is essentially vernacular mindset.

Discoveries that worked quickly spread and were copied and used for more innovation. There is usually one interesting feature in a Camp Ground that marks it as different from others. It may be a spectacular location, a bridge spanning a chasm with names of everyone in the camp listed on it. It might be a grotto, an Inspiration Stump in the woods, a lake, a unique layout, a unique cottage or style. This underlies the continuous fascination that we have for them: the sense of place.

On that complex armature of community pattern (the plan), there are buildings, whether called tents or cottages. The tabernacles or arbors and the few large scale dorms or activity buildings complete the picture. The spaces between buildings is as important as the buildings themselves.

HOW THE COTTAGES WERE INTEGRATED WITH THE PLANNING.

From the earliest days, the arrangement of the tents and then cottages was that the entry was toward the speaker or pathway and was always formal with the back of the tent given over to cook fires and informal behaviors. People listened to speakers and greeted visitors at the front of the tents and the tendency toward elaborate displays of detail is most often seen there.

Often the back sides of the cottages produce a secondary pathway that is livelier than the formal front side. The canvas tent era and some of the early cottages seemed to envision a sort of tableau of a family sitting area starting at the front of the tent, whether just a decorated area or a porch, and with tent subdivided with a back room for informal activities and sleeping. The earliest camps saw the invention of the whole integrated form.

Camp Meeting Grounds inevitably started with tents, still found at Ocean Grove, but there were other tent experiments. In West Branch, near Loch Haven, PA, a camp destroyed eventually by a flood and never rebuilt, there is an interesting print (pp.12,16) that

Above left, Grotto and well, Hedding Camp, N.H., central wells reinforced community. Well is at lower left of photo.
Left: Central arbor or tabernacle, Mt. Pleasant, N.C. Tabernacle has been restored, original was built 1830.

nows an entire encampment of two-story canvas tents, set up
almost like theater sets. My best idea is that these were built as
hed frames with a sleeping loft, covered over with canvas, but the
isual impact is impressive, and I have never seen it repeated in any
ther camp history–yet. Historic reports describe this camp as very
opular, with train service, and so many visitors that they had to
top running Sunday trains.

Camp Ground planning was also generative design–another way to
efine it would be a process of "design, erase, improve"; a process
hat also relates to adaptation, new invention and changing times.
At first the campgrounds were completely driven by pedestrian
novement. Horses and wagons gave way to trains and motorized
ehicles. How Camp Grounds came to deal with modern plumbing
nd the advent of electricity also changed the form. Often the
ew technical breakthroughts removed some of the communal
xperience, such as common wells or even common latrines.
Electricity can end up bringing good things, like refrigerators, but
ir conditioning can drive people indoors.

Pathways had to negotiate slopes and connect with the activity at
the center and this affected campsite layouts but roads tended to
be made with larger equipment and often created problems. In
amps like Bayside, in ME, highly crowned gravel roads defied the
normal slope of the land and the gridded streets run straight up
nd down. This grid did not get revised and the run-off in a storm
s significant. Some inventive solutions emerged to handle runoff.
Often roof gutters projected rainwater that was carried in stone
drains. Mt. Tabor, in New Jersey, is actually a small mountain with
oads that run up and down more than following the topography.
This makes for dramatic runoff and improvisation to get across
gutters that seem uncommonly deep when the rain is not falling
and overflow in the kind of cloudbursts that are common to middle
New Jersey.

The large camp meeting at Oak Bluffs, Martha's Vineyard also
shows the signs of a smaller layout that grew, developed several
sub "places" linked by complex pathways. Though vehicles can
drive on most of the roadways there, at certain times parking is
not allowed and cars are usually left at the perimeter. This is a
place where being in a car is a diminished experience compared to
walking anyway. That effect derived from its pre-vehicle, pedestrian
oriented design and it important to compare it with Ocean Grove,
Malaga, or any of the later 19th century site plans.

The spatial experiences at Oak Bluffs are varied and surprising.
What holds this large site together are the predominant porches
that allow pedestrian community. Once a year on Illumination
Night (third Wednesday of August), all the Cottages are lit with
lanterns, illuminated by everything from candles to LED lights. At
the finale of the summer's last program, the oldest person in the
camp gets to light the first lantern and then all the cottages are lit,
making for an evening stroll that is magical. Ritual plays a part as
well as form.

THE WATER, PLUMBING AND THE POWER

It is important to understand the multiple activities that built

Above: back of cottage space. Below side connections and back spaces form informal gathering places and connecting spaces.

Below: Illumination night, Wesleyan Grove, Martha's Vineyard at Forest Circle. Lanterns can be silk, paper or glass and are sometimes hand made.

community in camps. Besides the varieties of spaces from intimate and private to public, there were many daily interactions that made community a constant factor, to adjust, to improve or to resolve.

One of the basic requirements for planning a camp meeting ground was a "bounteous water supply. There are old cautions that if the water supply is "not great" "to locate large water tanks as a congregation of several thousands will consume an amount of water entirely incredible to persons not experienced in the matter." This advice from Gorham's *Camp Meeting Manual* doesn't reflect what was done everywhere. In many camps there are wells, and in one, a grotto to a spring. Meeting at the well or grotto for one's daily water was yet another layer of community activity.

A woman I met at one camp reported that she complained to her husband about the cold water only. He was a long term camp meeting member, and she was going to install a hot water tank. Her husband said that part of his childhood experience was that everyone carried water each day and she should be grateful that there was now running water. This dates running water in that camp to about 1985.

In South Carolina, the oldest camp ground I have visited, Cattle Creek, circa 1786 has its own large water tower, though the water is only fed to wooden cottages via a single tap. That camp has regular flush toilets in the wood cottages with their dirt floors. These are all active Camp Grounds.

Latrines are a much different issue. The historic accounts do not mention this, but every Camp Ground has had to deal with this, and modern health rules have been a poor match for the density of camps. In some locations there have been a running battles with local building departments to force upgrades. in Sterling, MA, a home owners' association was formed expressly to be able to get state and federal funds for shared leaching fields for the 1854 era camp

The older Southern Camps vary. Some have indoor plumbing but a number have either individual privies or remote group facilities, so that at any time of the day or night people are trekking to the bathrooms located at the perimeter of the camp. Whether this makes for a more social camping experience is not clear, but as an organizational matter, when there are combined facilities or privies these are located at the outer edges of the camp grounds. In the case of Indian Field, circa 1795, there are 99 wood cottages or tents in a complete circle and 99 wooden privies in another circle beyond, across the roadway, each with a certain individuality and an undeniable typology.

The provision of electricity has worked to affect the experience too. In Rock Springs, a continuously operated camp since 1794, there is power to all the wood tents, but only 20 Amp service each. This was a decision made consciously at the time, only 30 years ago. The life of the camp depends on people being outside, walking, sitting on porch swings, and visiting. Providing enough power for air conditioning would have pulled people away from the community experience, something I experienced in the height of a humid, 97 degree late afternoon. There was enough power for

Left above: a line of privies rings Indian Field Camp Meeting, an 18th century camp.

Left below: Rock Springs Camp Meeting, with only 20 Amp electric service which does not support air conditioning. The result of this lack of power is much more visiting and walking at night, see far right. The single light bulbs create a lantern-like quality. The wooden slats instead of windows is because ventilation is needed as well as privacy, but a view is not necessary.

ns, a few light bulbs, and small refrigerators but little more.

Camps with enough power for air conditioning there is less
cializing. Neshoba County Fair Grounds, a non-religious Fair
round that follows the spatial rules for Camp Meetings, has so
uch air conditioning that the form there is of a first floor that
open and has social activity with second and even third floors
mpletely windowless, as fully air-conditioned dorms. Some
ould say that there is activity enough there a ground level, and
e air conditioning is a necessary relief; but it does affect the look
d function of the place.

Vebsites for some of the rural South Carolina Camps celebrate the
ility to bring families to a place away from modern technology
order to experience a life where visiting, children and play still
ominate in a modern world. They talk about a way for parents to
et to know children better; they talk about rediscovering simplicity
d community.

*bove and above right: windowless air conditioned sleeping floors in Neshoba
ounty Fairgrounds. Right: the entertainment side of the street, note blank
all above "tent" on left of picture.
elow: Rock Springs: left rough kitchen with a single cold water faucet and
ight, Rock Springs at night--like a linear glowing lantern.*

Interior pedestrian street - Happy Hollow with sawdust spread for walking

Shared space at Neshoba Cty Fairgrounds showing layers of space.

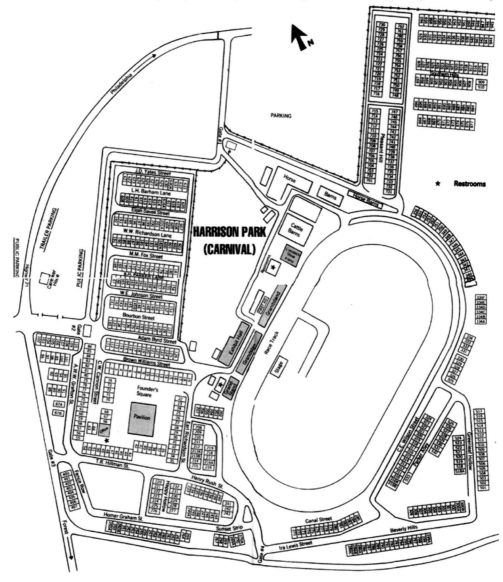

Neshoba County Fair Grounds, MS. This Fairground was always intended as a fairground, but the original form, seen in the lower left corner was typical of a Camp Meeting. The Fair was started in 1889 but most of its growth took place in the 20th century. The form of the Fairground follows the same kind of layout as a good Camp Meeting with narrow pedestrian ways and dense cottage layout by formal rules on set lot sizes, protection of trees, resulting in many complex types of spaces that create opportunities to meet up and strengthen bonds of community. The 20th century development of the form here in Neshoba also shows an organized way of dealing with automotive traffic, separating cars from pedestrians. The Fairground also features many areas, such as the racetrack, midway and exhibit buildings that are not common to Camps but are integrated well here. Neshoba County Fairgrounds functions as a private Land Trust.

Above: Ladders act as emergency egress equipment, necessary with windowless rooms on second and third floors.

Above: Back decks overhang a creek

Below: Large cottages around the race track using a lot of power. See transformer and wiring. Note wide stairs for socializing.

Originally a Ticket Booth in Hedding Camp, this cottage has been moved and converted to a residence. Moving cottages was a common occurrence and one of the powers of the Camp Meeting Association to reinforce rules and regulations. One leased a "tent site" but owned what sat on it. So if the rules were violated, one could be forced to remove one's "tent" or cottage. This was easier before plumbing and electricity, but also reflects the rugged charactor of a small cottage.

CHAPTER 3 -- LAND TRUSTS AND GOVERNANCE

and ownership has been a tenet of American government, especially a key concept recognized by the majority of Scots-Irish that were early participants in Camp Meetings. While the very first camps were often on rented land, the permanent camp meetings were almost universally organized as Land Trusts, usually chartered through state legislatures.

Historically, a group of investors raised the money to buy a plot of land for the purpose, and established the rules for the land trust and laid out a system to lease camp sites to individuals. In such an agreement, the land was owned by the association with campsites leased. In the early days, tents would have been erected on the campsites, but in time, these were replaced with permanent cabins, cottages, or as they are still called in the south, tents. The term "arbor" came from early preaching stands covered with tree boughs arranged for shade.

The New Jersey camp grounds that exist today were laid out during or just after the Civil War, and they reflect the changed times. Chartered as "religious municipalities" in the 19th century, these camp meetings were clearly towns and the concepts for laying out a camp meeting became more complex as commercial areas and municipal services such as libraries, fire and police departments were added.

Ocean Grove kept a Land Trust form of land ownership as a religious non-profit, so that land is leased, in a 99 year lease while a cottage is owned by a person and taxed by the town of Neptune.. The annual lease fees are based on the original lease and some pay as little as $25 a year, but newer leases may cost much more. These

fees support the many summertime activities. It is significant that this camp still erects 114 tents each year in the traditional way. These rental tents are taxed as income producing property and are not covered in the tax-free protection of the larger 501 (c)3.

The township of Neptune collects taxes on the cottages and owns the streets, a few parks and detention ponds. The Fire Department is located on land that is owned by Ocean Grove. The sidewalks are the responsibility of cottage owners. The Pavilion on the boardwalk is used for religious ceremonies and is not taxed; Ocean Grove owns the boardwalk. Besides the summer rental tents other commercial endeavors run by the Camp Meeting are taxed. It's an unusual arrangement that, surprisingly, seems to work well.

Responsibility for building changes and their approvals seems to rest with the Camp Meeting, it is unclear how far the Camp Meeting Association's approval power goes with regard to building codes, but this is a camp meeting where a good deal of restoration and new building occurs.

The utilities in the street, the maintenance of those streets, fire and police service are the responsibility of Neptune township. The Camp Meeting Association with the few commercial exceptions, pays no taxes. So most land and its use is controlled by the Camp Meeting; most services are not. Literally, the top of the street curb is the domain of the cottage owner, the bottom of the curb (street0 is the City of Neptune's concern. This creates an interesting situation. It seems to be an exercise in subsidiarity that gives control to those most invested in the land or service. It separates town services from land use. Zoning will be controlled through the historic district that is Ocean Grove. Neptune itself is larger than the square mile that is Ocean Grove, but Ocean Grove is a significant area within it.

Ground leases for residential properties are very unusual in real estate. There are no 'standard' Multiple Listing Service categories to reflect that condition of ownership, hence, one finds advertised lots "for sale." Technically, what is owned are the *improvements* on the lot. In practice, the renewable 99-year leases, (whose right to renew can be passed along), allow the homeowner to 'control' that

Above: Police station near the Temple at Ocean Grove Camp Meeting Ground, Neptune, NJ. Building is in keeping with the cottages in the area. Right: Mt. Tabor, NJ, has the Volunteer Fire Department located under the Tabernacle building that opens on an upper plaza. Steep slopes enable double use with civic uses sharing space with the tabernacle, and a commercial street us behind the public square.

Above left: Mt. Tabor's Tabernacle as viewed from the upper level on the "circle". Above right: the Post Offie in the same Tabernacle building, lower level, adjacent to the Fire Department. Below right: an outbuilding opposite the Fire Department in Mt. Tabor.
Bottom: Mt. Tabor Branch Library, one of two octagonal public buildings facing the Tabernacle.
Since these New Jersey Camp Grounds were established as "religious municipalities," they were always considered as complete places.

ot, just as a restaurant would control a highway pad site with a 20 ear ground lease.

he Land Trust has worked well for Ocean Grove. There are ifferent options in locations like Plainville, CT, where the land trust s set up as a recreational non-profit. Though the land is therefore on-taxed with the cottages owned, a legal ruling with the town as led to a situation where only a few cottages can be used year ound and that right is inherited. If no one is designated to carry on wnership of a designated cottage, the right to live there year round s lost. This seems to be in response to concerns from the town bout loading ballot boxes, and the seasonal restriction is found ommonly in the northeast. The result is that the cottages, with he exception of the handful that can be lived in year round are only vailable from April-October.

Why this matters is that when a large assortment of interesting tructures is left untended for many months, all sorts of damage an happen, from fire to storms to vandalism. This limitation on abitation is not unusual. The opposite can also occur when a own wants to take advantage of the property to create a place for ffordable housing and tear out or destroy old structures to install ew, unrelated and cheap housing. The Land Trust if it continues to xist can resist that change.

terling Camp, MA, became Waushacum Village Homeowner's Association recently and was able to access state funding and federal ural funding to build a group waste treatment septic field. This omeowner's association may be an intermediary condition between land trust and condominium. Because most campgrounds were riginally land trusts, there are a number of commonly held utilities nd other resources that could only be resolved through finding overnance systems that address those issues.

When a land trust is rewritten into a condominium, control over lesign, scale and size is usually the first casualty. Camps that have ept the Land Trust form and moved toward Historic Register or andmark status have better protections, though sometimes the and Trust itself is the problem.

In some cases cottages are handed down for generations and when suddenly an owner cannot be found, the Land Trust has no mechanism in place to reclaim the cottage. In other cases where the land trust is a religious 501(c)3, efforts must be made to maintain that status. New buyers must meet requirements such as church membership in order to buy.

In Monteagle Assembly, TN, anyone who has a lease is automatically a member of the governing association, and as such must be a member of a church. Because of this, the interpretation has been made that no cottage can be financed via a mortgage. Why? Because, in the case of a foreclosure, the bank would become, *defacto*, a member of the governing association – with the requirement for church membership -- an impossibility. This limitation on mortgages has worked well there and cottages are in good shape and well used, always a critical way to see how these very old land trusts are working today. The rules that govern owning in a campground have an equivalent to buying into a co-op building--a board has to approve a new owner who must meet a set of requirements.

A few Land Trusts have been able to institute a restriction that if a cottage owner does not show up for 3 years, the cottage–the property, is claimed by the Land Trust. Abandonment is one of the problems with 99 year leases. In a 99 year lease there is little that can be done legally if an owner just vanishes. In some camps there are variations on the lease terms–some are 25 years which becomes more manageable. Wesleyan Grove on Martha's Vineyard has only annual leases which allows a great deal of control over what renovations can be done and what materials used. Historically, a person could be ejected from a Camp Meeting Ground for violation of the rules, and that person would be required to move his cottage; often over the course of a night. This might have been

Below: this historic Camp Meeting organized itself into a homeowners's association in order to access federal and state funds to build a shared wastewater treatment field. The field is located on downhill property adjacent to the densely settled cottage streets. Adequate septic systems are an ongoing problem in many older camps where regulations have become stiffer.

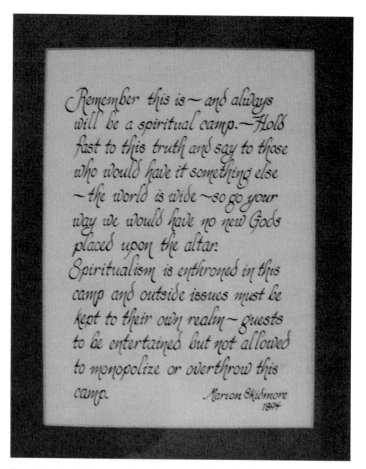

Remember this is ~ and always will be a spiritual camp. ~ Hold fast to this truth and say to those who would have it something else ~ the world is wide ~ so go your way we would have no new Gods placed upon the altar. Spiritualism is enthroned in this camp and outside issues must be kept to their own realm ~ guests to be entertained but not allowed to monopolize or overthrow this camp.

Marion Skidmore 1894

In active Camp Meeting Grounds, the conditions for being a member often include a strong reliance on tradition, as seen in this calligraphic statement at Lily Dale.

done by rolling the cottage over poles using a team of horses or oxen. One thing that is common is that cottages get moved. In some areas, there are neighborhoods created outside the Camp Meeting where moved cottages found new sites.

One of the most stringent Land Trusts is for Lily Dale Assembly. This camp meeting in western New York State is also the national headquarters of the Spiritualist Church. There are a number of permanent residents as well as an active summer season population. It has a few derelict cottages, probably due to the requirements for ownership which are complex. First, a potential purchaser must have been a member of the Spiritual Church for a number of years, and then have come to Lily Dale for two years and become known. Finally, in order to purchase, a potential buyer must agree to put in a number of volunteer hours a year, possibly as a medium. What results is a tightly committed community but difficulty with finding buyers for cottages.

Generally, in most operating Land Trusts with membership requirements, cottages remain affordable. How affordable? Cottages on the north shore of Boston, or near trendy areas in Connecticut, can be as low cost at $10,000-$30,000. Of course, the units are small, usually not winterized, and "fixer-upper" is a common hobby, plus one must pass requirements to be a member. Most people are active in programs during the smmer season in these communities and that is the attraction to owning a cottage there.

Below: Ongoing maintenance and repair is necessary but the size of the project is generally manageable, Bethel Camp, Haddam, CT.

Campgrounds that have been sold off or made into condos, costs generally rise. In good vacation locations, they may be very expensive. It is unclear if the degraded camps, where cottages have had their trim covered, vinyl siding applied and control lost over quality, are losing value. When the aesthetic appeal of a coherent set of structures is lost, the relatively small size and cheap appearance of the resulting cottages must depress value. The clashes of scale in some of these locations can be extreme and the results bizarre.

Certainly when the feel of community is damaged, a small, devalued cottage will be competing with ordinary housing in the immediate market area.

The Land Trust has evolved over time and can still be a valuable tool to create and maintain community and affordability. There are commercial land-trust type facilities often set up for retirement communities in which one leases the land for a monthly fee that includes landscape and maintenance but the structure, whether a double wide trailer or "Park Model" is owned separately. If a true land trust Camp Meeting were to be attempted today, the most important aspects after establishing a workable system of governance would be setting up the layout to reinforce the sense of community, looking for a generative approach to infrastructure so that it can respond to change, and establishing a way to guarantee the continued structural integrity of cottages, whether the threat is abandonment, fire, natural disaster, or disrepair.

A Land trust should retain approval rights on appearance of new construction, ideally through generative patterns for scale and siting. There should be written standards. Alliance with a municipality

The problems:
Left: When Laurel Park, in Northhampton, MA, became a condominium, design controls were lost with renovtions that damage the historic character of the Camp Meeting. This must result in lost real estate value as aesthetics decline.
Upper right : Cottage in Laconia, NH, a popular vacation site show cottages with fake stone and vinyl exteriors and detailing removed or covered over.
Lower, middle, also Laconia, complete disregard for scale and character of this older camp, where good older cottages remain, though threatend.

the Land Trusts become advantages to the municipality, such as reduced responsibility for land use regulation, maintenance or construction. This could be reflected in controlled infrastructure requirements and balance within the tax base due to density. A Land Trust should offer enough efficiency, be lean enough that the infrastructure and services would allow for low cost cottages paying low taxes.

The ideal Land Trust would keep structure costs and taxes low by absorbing demands for town services. Potentially Land Trusts could be created around existing property as well as greenfield properties. The intent should be to achieve a lean way of living that relies on community, reduced costs for dwellings, and a commitment to subsidiarity in shared responsibility and decision making.

In some ways a trailer park is a later version of a campground, with a relatively cheap hook-up charge for utilities, a simple and compact layout, and a usual situation of an individual owning a trailer instead of a cottage. The translation of this would involve a different type of dwelling, but using the examples of the campgrounds, or other

Below: part of the Commercial Area of Ocean Grove Camp Meeting, Neptune, NJ, where the land is part of the trust and the buildings are owned by individuals, paying taxes to Neptune, NJ. A working Land Trust.

non-residential structures and areas could be included, the critical difference between either the commercial retirement land trust or a commercial trailer park is the value inherent in self-governance. And successful self-governance relies on a developed sense of community.

What is the advantage to the municipality to have a land trust, no to mention a non-profit entity? The ability to tax the cottage itse offers value when this is offset by the density of the development. The organization of the Trust to control land use can reduce town government costs that deal with land use. Government is streamlined, potentially. Small cottages will have lower tax for an individual owner to pay, but in the aggregate there are more cottages per acre which should balance out the reduced value of th Trust itself. The new trend toward "Tiny Houses" would work we in a new Land Trust format. These houses, often self-built, reflect the need for people to be able to build according to the HUD/Ansi Codes that allow for smaller dwellings.

It is important to realize that Camp Grounds were also intentional communities with shared values and shared goals. This needs to be understood as part of the essence of long-lasting Land Trust Communities as well.

Typical older Gothic style cottage from Wesleyan Grove, Martha's Vineyard, showing platform base which made cottages easy to move and relocate. This is a transitional example with just a suggestion of a porch and still reflecting the original canvas tent styles where the scalloped rake trim suggest the old canvas double-fly tent.

CHAPTER 4 -- THE COTTAGES

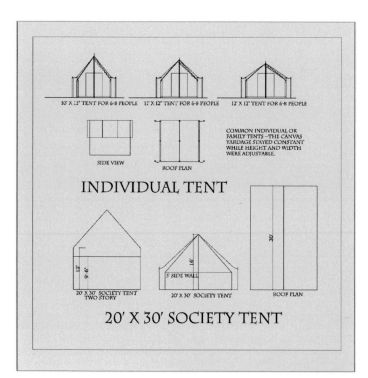

COMMON INDIVIDUAL OR FAMILY TENTS —THE CANVAS YARDAGE STAYED CONSTANT WHILE HEIGHT AND WIDTH WERE ADJUSTABLE.

10' X 12' TENT FOR 6-8 PEOPLE   11' X 12' TENT FOR 6-8 PEOPLE   12' X 12' TENT FOR 6-8 PEOPLE

SIDE VIEW   ROOF PLAN

INDIVIDUAL TENT

20' X 30' SOCIETY TENT TWO STORY   20' X 30' SOCIETY TENT   ROOF PLAN

5' SIDE WALL

20' X 30' SOCIETY TENT

WHAT MAKES IT A CAMP MEETING COTTAGE?

The most typical cottage is 12'-4" wide by 24'-28' long. What is surprising is that the 12'-4" dimension is found in camps from Maine to the Carolinas, in free standing cottages as well as wooden "tents" in rows found in the very old camps in North Carolina. This may be a direct result of rules found in the 1854 "Camp Meeting Manual" which laid out a 12' wide family tent that would have boards (imagine 2" thick) nailed to the outside of the side posts, 3 per side, 5' high. The ridge pole and front and back center poles were anchored and tied in with a precise requirement of just 40 yards of "factory" cloth Stretched over the frame to make the tent. The width, height and pitch of roof were organized by the forty yards of cloth requirement for an individual tent. These proportions were expanded for the construction of group or society tents where each group or family provided an amount of canvas for the larger tent. The typical size was 20' x 30', and when wood cottages were built for society use they were about that size, except two story cottages.

In Ocean Grove Camp Meeting, 114 canvas tents are still set up each year, very similar to the original design illustrated in the 1854 Camp Meeting Manual. Over time, the tent structure has gained some permanent infrastructure in the form of the wooden platform and shed at the rear of the platform containing kitchen and bathroom facilities and perhaps a convenient storage area for canvas, off season. Pictures of this are found in the chapter on Planning. The sides of the canvas tents are lashed to wooden posts and beams which remain off-season. The tent is typically a double-fly roof with traditional scallops hanging from the upper canvas. This scalloping evolved to become the decorative rake or barge boards that are typical of most Northeast wooden cottages.

The transition from canvas tent to wooden tent happened over time. In some cases the canvas walls were first replaced with wood and the canvas roof remained. "The Camp Meeting Manual" says that the canvas tops were less subject to leaks and they certainly gave more light to the interior. Eventually the cottages became all wood. The solid form cottage had a direct evolution from its factory cloth origins.

Foundations? Once the cottage in the north had become a wood structure, it became common to move them and cottages were meant to be movable. The first cottages were built either on post foundations or the floor beams were laid directly on the ground, as recommended in The Camp Meeting Manual, on leveled ground with flat laid wood strips perhaps 2' apart. Some older cottages still show a neat platform under the building. Before porches were widespread this platform served as a seating area.

Breeze reveals ridge beam supporting lower canvas with straps and upper canvas on metal posts through grommet holes. Note side posts with ropes supporting the horizontal load. Ocean Grove, NJ

Left, Cottages bear a close resemblance to nearby tents in Ocean Grove. These show the typology as it transitions from tents to cottages.

In the south the opposite occurred: after the initial canvas tents and wagons phase, the campground evolved into fixed site plans, where "tents" had dirt floors and were attached to other tents, moving them became difficult. At the same time, these tents do not share common walls, so the ownership is still understood as individual. Also these structures may have had less value because of the short camp meeting times in the south, usually a few weeks that reflected a time when farmers could leave their fields. In the north the concept that one owned the cottage and leased the campsite was clearer and the camp meeting season was usually six months. There are stories of a member being voted out of the campground for a rule infraction and made to move a cottage overnight. His campsite lease was cancelled. This happened recently in Wesleyan Grove, though the cottage, with utilities, was not moved.

Southern camps often have dirt floors, which can be covered with straw or sawdust with structure sitting directly on the dirt-unless modern upgrades have resulted in concrete slabs. Sometimes both examples are found in the same campground. In steeply sloping campgrounds, posts or brick piers are in evidence. In later years, people have installed continuous foundations, rotted sills have been replaced, and sometimes the entire cottage or tent has been placed on a simple concrete slab. That cottages come to slope and lean and yet stand for hundreds of years is also clear, but foundation failure is one of the first threats to structural stability.

Size also varies from small to the very small. In the "rule" of 40 yards of cloth, a 10' wide tent could be constructed with a steeper roof and that idea is found in a unique group of 10' wide cottages, and a few even narrower. Occasionally there are add-ons that are 6' or 8' wide, and one cottage in South Seaville, NJ. looks deceptively large with wide verandas, but is just 9'-6" wide. Consistency of scale within the campground seems to be how this is conveyed.

Above right: the Promenade at Rock Springs Camp Meeting.
Above middle: around the center ring of Indian Creek Camp Meeting, SC, note detail of porch support.
Right: Promenade at Balls Creek Camp Meeting with more bright colors.
Below: Swings ready for camp opening at Balls Creek.

Somehow these very small cottages seem to feel right. It is rare for a cottage wider than 24' to "feel" correct. Generally roof pitches become compromised, either becoming flatter or looking ungainly Twenty-four feet wide is a surprisingly small dimension for houses these days; it is the typical width of small bungalows that were popular in the middle decades of the 20th century. Seen in a row of Association Cottages, mostly 20' wide, these cottages look much grander than a 24' wide bungalow. A 16' wide cottage is rare in older camps, but larger cottages were built in the later 19th century as wealth became a factor and larger examples are common.

Today a camp meeting cottage has instant recognition because of the particular proportions and scale generated by the steep pitched roof, the balloon frame, and the relationship between floors, roof and windows. The thrifty use of materials, a blend of practical availability and simple detailing is also essential in understanding the cottage. Decoration that looks extreme is usually based on a desire for a level of ecstatic expression that remains based in simple execution and a lot of creative thought.

Except for unusual linear camp grounds in North Carolina or the "dog-trot" style cottages found in Mississippi, it is nearly universal that the principal gable of a cottage faces the street–very much like a formal statement or expression about one's place in the community. Though there are examples of "L" shaped cottages and later Victorian large cottages that defied the rules adding turrets and complex facades, addressing the street is still the predominant concept. Porches, layers of separation between public and private space are part of that statement. When the majority of the camp meeting follows the rules, the occasional variant still works, even enhances the spirit of individual expression within the limits of the community of cottages.

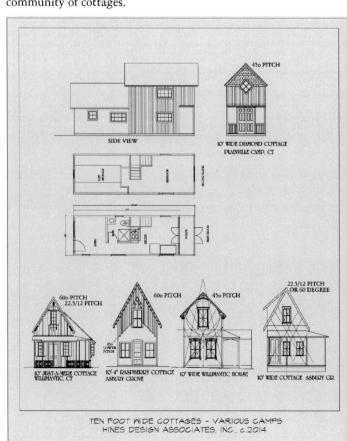

TEN FOOT WIDE COTTAGES - VARIOUS CAMPS
HINES DESIGN ASSOCIATES, INC., c.2014

10' wide "Diamond" cottage, Plainville, CT, plan and elevations are shown left page.

These are simple structures, lean in execution yet containing a level of complexity that is satisfying. Sometimes there is ingenuity in construction or an attention to mathematical details that give them balance and order. In trying to draw up one of these cottages, I have come to realize how precise these proportions are. This opens the question of whether there is a transition point between a classical style with attention to proportion or simple vernacular thinking. It is worth considering the beginning stages of cottage design.

The early 19th century cottages were made from simple timber frames, one post at each corner and one midway on each side–this matched the canvas tent dimensions. Since camp sites were laid out on canvas tent sizes, this meant the wood cottages had to fit. They were balloon framed with the loft level around 9'-4" or about halfway from ridge to floor, and the plate, where the roof rafters sit, attached at 12'-4", almost without exception, regardless of width of the cottage. I have mentioned this to some people who live in these places and the answer I get is the lean one: it was a typical length that wood was available in at the time. There is efficiency to that.

Some of the finish design detailing with upper siding overlapping lower siding was no doubt due to the length of available wood to run from ridge down the front gable. In remote locations getting any large or heavy materials would have increased difficulty and cost.

Ten foot wide cottages. upper left: Tiny beige cottage recently demolished, Willimantic Camp Meeting, Note roof pitches and windows. "Just-A-Mere" Cottage, Willimantic Camp Meeting, and Asbury Grove raspberry pink cottage below.

The Wigwam Cottage, Hedding Camp, NH, with a 10' wide cottage plus 6' wide kitchen in front, interior of that kitchen on right.

The timber frame was sided with vertical tongue and groove siding, cut from a kind of hard pine where the sap dried and hardened to make these 1" thick walls extremely strong. This single thickness of siding is often seen on the interior partitions as well. A small trim cleat anchors the boards at the floor and ceiling.

The skill of carpenters at finding ways to use smaller sizes of lumber is an example of lean building that challenges us today. The chapter on Details captures more of these examples.

Even when that original thin vertical siding was varied with board and battens or whatever was available, the vertical aspect of the cottage was part of the look. This is reflected in windows, roofs and even the massing itself. Shingles and clapboards were a later material.

Roofs often were constructed with purlins perpendicular to rafters with roofing applied directly to them with no sheathing layer. In the south this helped in ventilating the upper floors as a breeze

Interior of the Diamond Cottage showing roof purlins. Diamond window hinges up and can be hooked open with a screen door hook on the rafter.

could be generated. Exposed rafters are a common look. In some southern cottages with tin roofs, people have begun to add solid foam insulation sheets to the underside of the roofs resulting in a decided difference between the insulated version and the infrared radiation from the unprotected metal roof. In the chapter on Southern camps, we will discuss the way the slatted walls generated air circulation.

Windows, generally double hung, were mounted to the inside of the walls with trim applied, only if necessary, to the exterior. In the simplest examples the siding was cut out for the window and retained as an off-season shutter. In some areas the Gothic rounded or pointed top windows were popular. Whether the Camp Meeting Cottage was a cross between a chapel, a house and a tent is hard to say, but ideas about building were exchanged between town and campground. Muntin bars in window were simple, though inclusion of stained glass or unusual patterns is not unusual. A two- over-two type window is most common unless

Upper left: 11' wide sections make up a larger L-shaped house, Asbury Grove; upper right: 10' wide cottage, Willimantic; left: cottage in Hedding Camp, NH,
Below: A common cottage type: porch, double height section and added on informal additions, kitchen, bath to the rear, Asbury Grove.

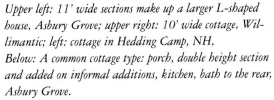

some special window has been chosen for the front. Sometimes window trim existed simply to hold the shutters on.

There was a warning in Rev. Gorham's 1854 work, "The Camp Meeting Manual", about creating places that resembled "shanty towns". Though one can argue that over time, poor maintenance and bad design decisions have evoked that image, building a shanty town or slum was not the intention. What could be accomplished with lean thinking and thrifty design could be beautiful.

These cottages were built, at a minimum, as shelter. Over time and with money, people fixed them up and added decoration. The basic cottage is recognizable in most campgrounds in the north. A small box-like 2 story cottage with various add-ons such as a porch, typically, and an assortment of smaller boxes in the back containing kitchen, bathroom and perhaps a hot water heater.

Then there are some of the organizational issues, such as public face toward the communal street or path or toward the central speaker area, and the functional area to the rear, where the cooking fires and latrines were established. The back of the tents at first and, later the cottages, was always the informal side and it had an entirely different and often lively life. This describes the dual nature of the community, spiritual and everyday.

In general, the most common roof pitch with a 12' wide cottages is 45 degrees or 12/12. Of course this varies and in some of the southern camps, the pitches are quite low, but within a camp all the pitches are similar. With the extremely narrow cottages the roof is usually close to a 60 degree pitch, and in those, the roof form approximates an equilateral triangle. It is unclear if the geometry relates to the religious concept of Trinity or if it is simply a pragmatic way to get more headroom upstairs.

It does reflect the initial advice about canvas tents—if a narrower tent was desired, the center ridge pole must be taller. This works out precisely with the advice to make the roof from 40 yards of canvas cut into strips. The 10 foot wide tent generates the 60 degree roof pitch, the equilateral triangle, the just barely adequate standing ceiling height on the sleeping floor.

Above: a History Cottage, Empire Camp, Poland, ME, an example of a preserved older cottage clearly demonstrating the original form of a tent, with wood platform and "scallops". Though it has a loft, this is what one-story cottages can look like.

Below: A one-story cottage in Plainville, Camp, CT, shows the lower plate height still supporting a sleeping loft that has a window down onto the porch. The simplicity of this shotgun type cottage relies on a good porch and social space. Only the front area is this elegantly detailed. It is otherwise a simple and efficient cottage.

Below: left, 10' wide cottage with equilateral triangle loft with added shed dormer, Asbury Grove.

STAIRS

Any close observer of building will begin to wonder how someone managed to get a stair in, and how the staircase for a 12' x 24' cottage did not dominate the design. The answer is that the stairs are steep, narrow, and intricately connected to the width, height and roof slope of the cottage. While any variety of layout can be found, straight or "L" shaped with plenty of winders is common. Codes today co not allow these stairs, but they continue to work.

The chapter on Details will explain the finer points of stairs, windows and structural innovation. See the diagram on balloon framing and stairs to the right.

Different Camps have their own types of Cottages and there are many rules that allow us to identify them as camp meeting cottages, but each camp ground also develops special details, rules or even massing ideas that are only found there.

Pitman Grove has a type that is found in large numbers there, but is rare elsewhere–the upper floor is larger than the lower floor and seems to float on a colonnaded porch. Some camps seem to have large double doors in the center of the cottage. People have suggested this was to assist with moving furniture in and out at the beginning of a season, but the tendency to have a wide-open first floor and more private upper floor is typical in most camps; the first floor was for socializing.

Lily Dale (NY) has a high number of "L" shaped houses, and Plainville, CT, has some very good one story examples.

In the southern camps which can seem identical when first encountered, there is a "code" for each that may have rules such as benches to the front or a covered walkway, or outhouses on the perimeter. In some areas in the south the "tents" may resemble

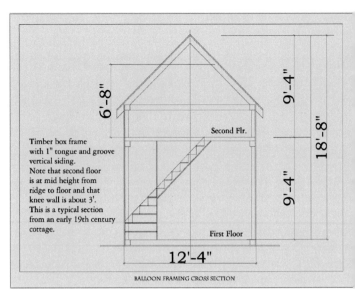

tobacco barns, elsewhere, stock pens, or the Southern dog-trot cottage with connecting breezeway. In most Northern camps, the style of handrails or amount of carving on barge boards can be the standout.

The cottages of Bayside, Maine have intricate geometric design of the siding itself and a tendency toward diamond windows. The feathery wood detailing in South Seagrove suggests the organic forms of trees.

When cottages get too large, they can cease to look like a Camp Meeting Cottage. In the case of the large cottage below, left, the building looks outsized, the roof becomes overwhelming. And yet, this cottage is only 24' wide, about the width of a typical 1920s era American Bungalow. The verticality has been compromised by the wide horizontal band. The cottage to the right feels much better.

Above: Big Cottage, Plainville, CT. with correctly scaled cottage to the right.

Right: medium sized cottage but with finer grained scale, verticality is maintained.

Left, typical Pittman, NJ, cottages seems to float on spindly posts allowing good cooling under the suspended second floor room.

Camp Faithful, Southington, CT, including the section from the circle, above, demonstrate a predominant use of large center double doors, a similar example is seen at Bethel Camp in Haddam, CT, both are Adventist Camps, but the double doors may also be a trend that was prevalent at the time these cottages were built. Styles help date cottages in that way..

55

Upper left, small "star"' ccottage from Lily Dale, NY, a Spiritualist Camp Meeting Ground. Above and below, sypical L-shaped larger cottages from this camp. Golf Carts are frequently used in Camp Meetings as cars are hard to fit into the dense layouts and are generally banished to the edges of the property.

Below: Large Lily Dale Cottage, probably winterized. This Camp Ground is near Buffalo, NY, and glassed in porches are more common, at least in the year-round cottages.

Above: abandoned cottage, Camp Etna, ME, demonstrating clapboards covering porch ceiling. To the side: 10' wide Johnson Manse Chapel, which includes an "L" shaped-stair at the back to an upper room Below Asbury Grove Cottage with rear cottage, taken over by the Camp Meeting Association and recovered from debilitated state. To see this in winter go to P.110

Dog-Trot form "tents" from South Union, MS and Old Lebanon, MS, below, showing a consistent style with a square window on each side of the enclosed sleeping areas and the center "trot" that connects the formal side to the back kitchen and eating areas which may be open or roughly fenced in as seen through the center of the cottage above. At South Union the tents are continuous and form an edge around the center Arbor or Tabernacle.

Note: Material possessions are simple enough that there is no need to secure these sites in the off-season. An unusual twist in a materialistic society: lean furnishing to the extreme.

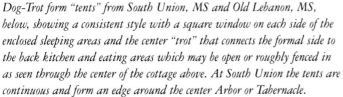

Right top: Cypress Methodist Camp, SC, with separate cottages and large live oak with Spanish moss. Windows are glazed here.
Middle and below, Indian Field Camp, SC, resembles a tight row of something akin to tobacco barns. Bottom right, single structure is tent #1 at Indian Field, the only one with a raised wood floor.

Though old and simple, these places, in season, are powerful examples of community. These camps date from the late 18th century.

58

Upper left: a typical Bayside type cottage with diamond windows.

Above: rear view of Penobscot cottage showing precise geometry of gable boards and trim of "broken-back" addition to allow for upper gable window. The geometry of this cottage is of a level of complexity that reveals itself when one tries to draw it. The half round battens and the interlocking circles are beautifully done. Inside the upper two levels are suspended by cables from the roof rafters, which will be discussed in the Detail Chapter.

Right above: Here the battens are triangular in section, a detail that can easily be set up to cut standard wood at 45 degree angles. In this case the height of the triangle is the same thickness as the upper boards so that the ridge is in the same plane as the upper vertical pieces.

Left and Right: this cottage is part of the Park Row at Bayside where camp site sizes were fixed and cottages built to the same size, yet are variations on a theme. Roof pitches and widths tie them together.

61

Besides the series of narrow 10' wide cottages there are a few designs that are extremely vertical for their base. One campground has a design for cottages that includes a tall square tower, found in several cottages. See Right, from Bayside.

Left and below: tall, narrow cottages, Lakeside, Belgrade Lakes, ME,
Right: one of several cottages at Bayside, ME, with square tower rooms attached.
Lower right: "Tall Timbers" which boasted uncut vertical siding full height of the cottage. Railings for the two balconies could not be replaced because current building codes would have required a 3' height, violating the historic design of closer to 18" in height.
This should be resolved by the 2005 designation of Wesleyan Grove as an Historic Landmark.
Far lower right: Tall tower type cottage at Wesleyan Grove, Martha's Vineyard.

COTTAGES WITH A VERTICAL FOCUS

What ties all these diverse cottage types together is the combination of focus on planning to create community, camp site size, and a sense of limits on design that also allow a high degree of individual expression within those limits. The critical factor is that the cottage design promotes community continuity and social connection while allowing lean space for living.

The "Vernacular" Cottages, Bayside, ME. The upper left cottage is the original version of this "vernacular" cottage, but that cottage was engineered into a set of plans, and one could order a copy built, with variations for layout, entry, windows, dormers, and decks. Three variations shown here exist at that camp. See Details chapter.

Right: South Seaville Campground, NJ where Civil War era cottages resemble branching trees and the streets are sand. A peaceful place with streets of sand.

Though the cottage below is a stand-out it also fits in with its community.

MT. TABOR, PARSIPPANY, NJ

Larger cottages often blend individuality of style with a lot more complexity in an ecstatic and optimistic level of decoration. The concept of lean seems to be at odds with these cottages but the level of decoration is often added over time using simple repetitive shapes.

Upper left cottage is an unusual example of a row house, facing the tabernacle area in Mt. Tabor, NJ, where the upper right cottages are located as well. Above is a porch built around trees, and there are many cottages here built on steep hills. Above right is a view of the core circle at Mt. Tabor facing the row houses.

Left upper corner and adjacent: striking red cottage that may have been cut back to accommodate a tree in the back.
Above: Gray Cottage, South Seaville, NJ
Below: a view of several cottages creating an ethearal lilac view of back yards and distant cottages, Asbury Grove, MA

Right: nearly matching pair with singular curving trim, alike but individual.
Middle right; a tiny cottage that has been added onto with an eclectic touch.
Below: lilac cottage left page bottom shown from front.

he cottages or tents shown here are far smaller than the average ouse today, Frequently their look is dramatically different from e average American house, while still providing a satisfying eling of home. In many ways this kind of house is as daring in sign statement as any modern glass box house. At the same ne, the scale and approachability of these houses establishes eir place in forming the community.

e size and simplicity of the houses is part of their leanness. nese houses are easy to maintain. When they are not andoned, they are maintained fairly easily. When you can lk out on a porch roof and paint the upstairs or paint it from e ground with a roller, the manageability of these houses ems scaled just right. The typical design of two rooms on the st floor and two on the second is frequently expanded, but the ea of a simple and manageable dwelling is the essence of the n cottage.

Left: complicated cottage from Round Lake, NY.
Above: a single cottage that looks as though it might be two, at Round Lake. These larger cottages that are still a manageable scale. The cottage above suggests an attempt to make a bigger cottage while keeping smaller scale.

CHAPTER 5 - DETAILS

Camp Meeting Grounds were built simply, with little money for extravagance at the beginning. The Camp Meeting structures became a rich source of thrifty detailing and ingenious vernacular invention. People loved the experience and the exuberance of the Camp Meeting experience, and this led to a tradition of decoration and embellishment. The language of community was spoken in the unique details that often copied and improved on preceding cottage design –the essence of vernacular design and innovation.

The decorative quality of Camp Meeting cottages often leads us to overlook the more important gift of innovative structural detailing. Some of these ideas may have been experimental or simply reflect true ingenuity in solving structural problems using the least amount of lumber, or combining metal cables and rods to solve design problems. This depth of understanding materials is often lost today to a habit of simply ordering pre-engineered and often expensive structural wood beams or fittings.

COTTAGE BASICS

Starting with the typical northeast cottage we find a number of critical pieces:

- Frame--originally tent poles but later timber frame
- Siding—originally vertical and thin, later adapted to other finishes. At first, canvas.
- The roof and its pitch – this becomes closely tied to head heights and stairs. A 12/12 pitch or 45° is common but steeper can be found.
- The gable – facing the street and symbolic of one's stance/representation in the community.
- Rake or barge boards, fascia boards, roofs.
- Windows, doors and casings
- Porches and platforms, often with unusual framing.
- Brackets –structural uses merge with decoration
- Railings, distinctive baluster designs posts, lathe turned or not, capitals for posts
- Skirting—that infill between the ground and the porch or house.

Above: The ornate Alpha Cottage at Craigville, MA, has all the elements that were common in cottages, though not always present in some simpler versions the Gothic window treatments are applied.

Below: a complex facade is composed simply of sticks arranged for expression.

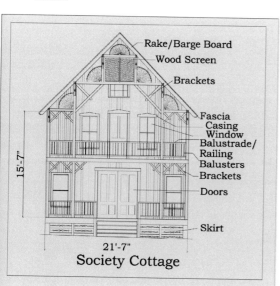

Rake/Barge Board
Wood Screen
Brackets
Fascia
Casing
Window
Balustrade/
Railing
Balusters
Brackets
Doors
Skirt

15'-7"
21'-7"
Society Cottage

Guide to various parts of a Society Cottage.

Abovue: Left cottage has a simple handrail that is also a structural member, a "K"truss with a vertical tension bar at the center. This truss can carry the porch and allows for very light wood framing. Right hand cottage uses brackets both structurally and decoratively to support the porch.

There are landscape features that include trestles to connect paths where the Camp ground has steep slopes or wooden sidewalks edging a street.

Complete schemes using basic themes are found with features copied from one camp to another. The Gothic style of cottage reflects carved and curved wood work, usually surface applied, but there are examples of even more complex window casing and head trim details that resemble shadow boxes. Pointed top gothic windows also suggest a chapel at the scale of a cottage.

STRUCTURE AS DETAIL

Details tended to make good use of materials and accomplished remarkable feats of structure with minimal materials. In Pine Grove a decorative balcony is actually a "K" truss supporting the balcony itself and decorative brackets brace a deck framed with very thin members. In another example cross bracing to keep the roof from splaying out is handled with a decoratively shaped structural cross piece. The potential to have decorative railings serve the purpose of structure, railing, and ornament is a valuable insight into lean building. The fact that these details have endured

for close to 150 years shows that the structural ideas behind them sound. In one camp, structural cottage bracing is done large-scale and visible on the exterior--a bold and effective touch.

BAYSIDE

Bayside, near Northport, Maine, has a collection of ingenious deta and some details that are the result of tightly organized geometry. A couple of cottages that I have seen have used metal tensioning rods to hang the upper floors of the cottages allowing the floor framing to be very light with spans allowing open space. A buildi that was used as a camp store has threaded rods and turn-buckles supporting central beams for two upper floors. It was reported th the balance of the tension rods and compression beams was strong enough that when the structure was knocked off its foundation in hurricane it was possible to pull it back on its foundation with the walls still plumb.

Penobscot Cottage (p.74) is very much a work of art. The 16' wic cottage has two upper floors suspended by rods from cross pieces at the rafters–a bit like an A-frame, or flat tripod. The center bea carries wood plank floors of the attic and second floor, dramaticall

Close-up view of truss-railing--center rod goes through a block and down, anchoring the strcture. Also of interest is the rafter tie, both necessary to hold the roof together and decorative as another example shows below.

educing floor to floor heights and allowing a compact, L-shaped tair. The skin of this cottage has been restored and reflects an intricate mathematical connection between round forms, triangles and rounded battens. Attempting to draw the subtle proportions, pitches, and terminations leaves one realizing that these simple ottages contain complex thinking.

A second cottage has a similar geometry. Bayside has a tradition of strong vertical battens, some round, some hexagonal, and some triangular, bias cut from square stock, an ingenious method for etting the look of a fine trim detail for little work beyond setting up a table saw or jigsaw to cut the 45 degree section. This cottage also has upper boards that overlap the lower boards and terminate a 45 degree chevrons that intersect precisely with the triangular beveled cut trim that are just about the same height as the overlaid boards. One of the lean geometries of many cottages is that, because wood lengths were limited, at gables the upper siding, always vertical, could overlap the lower siding with opportunities for interesting terminations and transitions.

The "Diamond Cottage", (Plainville, CT) shown in the chapter "Cottages". is another precise organization of proportions, including a diagonal set upper window that is hinged with a simple creen door hook to the rafters to hold it open.

ayside also marks one of the few camp grounds where an historical model was studied, replicated and offered for sale for hers wanting to have a new cottage based on original vernacular esign. These were built in the 1960s, post and beam with dvertisements that a cottage could come with front or side entry d various options for roof dormers. The four that were built emonstrate almost every possible variation on the original.

The Penobscot Cottage in Bayside has an unusual structural detail in which two floors are suspended via three metal rods from a cross piece tied to the rafters. This cottage is about 16' wide and this detail allows spanning with wood that is at most 6" deep plus the wood floor planking. This cottage also has an extremely complex geometry happening on the skin with relationships between vertical detailed boards, battens and circular terminations on the gable boards. I express special thanks to the late Tom Gavin, an architect who owned and renovated this beautiful cottage and showed me its secrets.

Far Left: Bayside's other rodded cottage has threaded turnbuckles that keep it tightly pulled together, see next page middle. This cottage was originally a general store with two floor above it.

Checkered panels open to a sleeping porch. Wood is stacked after winter's clean-up.

74

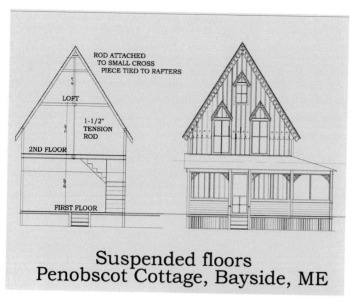

ROD ATTACHED TO SMALL CROSS PIECE TIED TO RAFTERS

LOFT

1-1/2" TENSION ROD

2ND FLOOR

FIRST FLOOR

Suspended floors
Penobscot Cottage, Bayside, ME

Left: threaded rods at another Bayside cottage--a former general store;
Above: Approximately 1" diameter suspension rod at Penobscot attic.

STAIRS

Any close observer of building will begin to wonder how someone managed to get a stair in, and how the staircase for a 12' x 24' cottage did not dominate the design. The answer is that the stairs are steep and narrow. While any variety of layout can be found, straight or "L" shaped with plenty of winders is common. These stairs are very much shoe-horned in, often conceived with a sure understanding of which foot will go where. Stairs as narrow as 24"-29" are common and risers 9"-10" are easy to find. The old formula of 2 risers + 1 tread adding up to 24"-25" still works here even when the tread gets reduced to 8" or even 7". Proportioning for stairs shows that when one must step higher the foot cannot comfortably go as far forward. The design of the stairs is constrained to having headroom when one gets to the top, and with the usual 3' or 4' kneewall, this means ending the stair closer to the middle of the upper room and working across and then along the outside wall from there. The winder stair illustrated below, also puts the top step closer to the center.

These tiny stairs, with the narrow width are surprisingly easy to use and difficult to fall from–though a challenge to move furniture, however I have seen double beds at the top of nearly impossible stairs. In some cases trap doors allowed furniture to be moved to the upper levels. Codes today would not allow these stairs, but they do meet often meet the dimensional requirements found in building codes for spiral stairs, just flattened out.

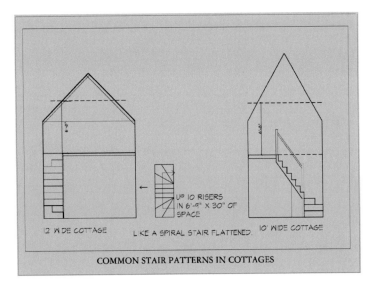

12' WIDE COTTAGE   LIKE A SPIRAL STAIR FLATTENED.   10' WIDE COTTAGE

UP 10 RISERS IN 6'-9" X 30" OF SPACE

COMMON STAIR PATTERNS IN COTTAGES

What becomes apparent is that the width of the cottage, slope of the roof, and design of the stair are intricately linked.

With a balloon framed cottage, usually with a 12'-4" top plate, where the rafters sit, the best headroom at the top of the stair is usually near the middle of the cottage. This means that the stair must end up there. The result is generally an "L" shaped stair—at least in the older, narrower cottages. Of course every variation on this rule is found. Some of the most successful of these tiny stairs have winders, at the top and bottom of the run so that there is headroom when one reaches the top step. Ten risers at 9" or so with a 7" tread is not uncommon.

Winders were often added at the landing with attention to where

each foot would be set. Nosings on the narrow treads are often not there.

It's not unusual to see a sliding window fitted into the framing at the stairs. These tend to be ventilation openings rather than glazed windows. Even in one of the big "society cottages" little space is expended on stairs. They are tucked into corners or are part of the separation of the front part of the cottage from the back kitchen

Above: It is possible that this stair was rebuilt to remove the top winders--thus leaving the landing with a low ceiling height. The lower winders have been replaced with a landing and the stairs now extend into the kitchen which not have been original, but under the stairs there is now room for a hot water heater. A lean adaptation Upper left, sliding window rides on horizontal girt in stair well.

Above, lower right and below, Willimantic Cottages incuding two examples of a sloped porch. This may have been a naive attempt to resolve a front orch with a side sloping porch, but the rocker at the low side of the porch ffers no problems when seated in it. Right cottage has been demolished.

area. Occasionally one finds a side oriented linear stair, but in general this cuts down on the usable width of the living room.

WILLIMANTIC

The Willimantic Camp Meeting has a number of inventions that are hard to find elsewhere. Some of them were simple attempts to resolve roof slopes on porches with unusual effects in which slopes resulted in simply lower ends of porches, low enough for sitting if not for standing. One of these was torn down after the first I saw it, and though the quality of this picture is not great, it is the only remaining record. There is one other similar example remaining in this camp, a few blocks away.

Willimantic has its share of tiny houses, as well. Those under 10' wide look remarkably "right sized" due to decreased sizes of elements such as windows and doors. "Just-a-Mere "cottage has a 28" wide by 6'-3" door and windows that look correct at 1'-8" wide. The porch rail here is just 18" high. More of these are being lost due to lack of funds to preserve them. The unusual one with the flatter roof (page 50)looked smaller and it may that roof slope is important to keeping the sense of scale right. This cottage is 10' wide with a 12' plate height (the height where the rafters are placed). This is typical of most 10' wide cottages except that on the beige cottage on P. 50, the roof slope is about 12 over 12. Most like the one to the left, are steeper if they are narrow.

Willimantic also has a number of examples of windows mounted flush to the inside of the vertical siding. This is an early convention seen in a number of camps. They follow the model of post and beam construction with tongue and groove vertical siding attached to it. Cutouts for windows were then made with the windows mounted to the *inside* of the siding. The siding becomes the trim—often just painted a contrasting color. Applied trim to windows was about decoration and limited to formal areas. Doors were done in much the same way. Any supporting members were simply attached to the inside of the exposed wall. This system is also found in Wesleyan Grove. This allows the bare bones of a window to be purchased.

WINDOWS

The earlier cottages ran the siding vertically with windows cut in later. The windows in the old style cottages were applied to the *interior* of the wall and often had no exterior trim. In a wall where there are no interior studs, these are timber framed with the siding spanning from top to bottom this kind of window is unusual. Sometimes a post is added to stabilize the window, and in larger structures, the windows are located near a structural post as well. The pulleys are visible on wood casings, the window unit look like little more than sash and a bounding box of wood. It is the most economical type of installation imaginable and even looking at it closely it is challenging to figure out the installation technique and how the simplicity could be duplicated with today' windows. With clapboards or shingles, window trim was necessar to terminate the boards, but with the vertical siding this was not the case. Convention required a semblance of trim, but it is just painted on. Actual decorative trim was added as ornament, and

Above: Fancy Gothic window with colored glass inset and double-hung operation. Applied trim as the window is mounted to the interior.

Above: A good example of an interior mounted window in a single thickenss wall. This detail is common in many camps. Exterior trim is sometimes added as only a decorative accent. Interior trim when there are only exposed wood studs makes for some simple detailing around doors and windows. This trim technique is also visible in the view to the left.

not necessary to finish the window installation.

Window flashing at the heads became another excuse for decoration or ornament, and the designs for these are an interesting assortment, from a simple piece of wood with some small brackets to hold them up, combined with a floor transition detail, to intricate trim details.

Sometimes windows are completely ignored and openings in buildings are just for ventilation, controlled by solid sections of siding raised on pulleys in what is otherwise seen as solid wall. This thinking re-opens the question of windows: for view or for ventilation? This discussion is repeated adamantly in the Southern Camps.

SIDING AND ROOFING

There are many variations on siding. Flush, vertical, tongue-and-groove siding were merely the most basic. When the tongue-and-groove siding is milled from hard pine, the sap in the wood acts o harden walls that would be to flimsy to support windows, but other techniques for minimal support also are found, such a a sysem of purlins or expansion of the timber frame. The one board thick detail often occurred on interior walls as well, with the vertical siding anchored by a simple cleat at the floor and ceiling.

Verticality was also expressed by board and batten siding with a different layer for the upper gable terminated creatively over the lower siding. These designs varied over time and patterns differ by camp. There were distinct styles, and there were evidently companies that sold certain trim patterns that can be found in a number of camps.

Siding and roofing come in many forms and sometimes are interchangeable. I have seen a shed roofed with miscellaneous

Ventilation is clearly seen as a separate issue from vision in creating openings in buildings. These small string and pulley systems are found frequently as ways to operate windows. Below is a sliding vent-only unit just under the plate, and almost at floor level. Both of these are from Plainville, CT.

Above: slits provide ventilation for this Southern Camp where privacy is more important than a view.

Above: window flashing by a board that is integrated with the exterior and rests on trim batten, supported by a tiny wood bracket.

Below: Sun shades in Boulder, CO, Chautauqua. Wood clapboard siding applied to thin sticks is simple and also allows air to get through acting as a wind spoiler to keep the shades from blowing off in high winds which are frequent in this mountain camp.

Above: a pair of windows mounted to the interior face of siding with trim added merely for decoration. Below: Winter window covers become sun screens and shutters. Bracing stick may be mounted to the window with hardware.

colored vinyl composition tiles, varieties of pressed boards, hurricane shingles, asphalt roofing as siding, slab wood scrap, clapboards as ceilings, and any number of inventions, trials and make-do applications. Since keeping the weather out of any cottage is essential to the survival of the cottage and therefore the Camp Ground, roofing is important, but as well, foundations can be the detail that fails and since these cottages were often moved, what is used for a foundation can vary. Sometimes it is just a fortunate find of a stone to set a cedar post on.

While the interior timber frame with vertical tongue and groove siding to the exterior is the norm, there are examples in Northampton, at Laurel Park, where the timber frame is on the outside and the single line of siding is to the inside. How the balloon framing works with this set up is unclear. There are other variations on the balloon framing that include more horizontal girts to carry the siding. In Camp Greene, RI, there are examples of horizontal sub-frame members at 4' heights, allowing them to use fairly standard lumber, 2x4 or less, with a siding that resembles typical bead board. This camp, mostly destroyed, has enough remnants of cottages to show a unique roof detail. There is evidence of metal straps that crossed over the ridge and were captured by a long metal stamped strip. The strip has been embossed with a floral detail and nails driven at the center of the flowers complete the look. Apparently this tied down some sort of sheet roofing, perhaps only building paper, but the anchoring system has outlasted whatever membrane was used, significantly providing a layer of floreate detail to the fascia and barge boards. Layers of old shingles are still visible, but the idea of a decorative metal roof system is something have not seen elsewhere.

Most southern camp meetings have gone to metal roofing, but asphalt is more common in northern camps.

SOUTH SEAVILLE

South Seaville, near Cape May, New Jersey, has details that seem to echo the trees and nature around it, making us look at the use of detailing to enhance Camp Meeting values about Nature by expressing it in the wood detailing that plays with light, shadow and the idea that a house is part tree in the most literal way. Some cottages here have intricate folded plate roofs with minimal roof framing members. Rafters are on the order of 2x3s with horizontal boards as sheathing. The result is a roof plane that seems almost paper-thin.

Looking up at folded plate roof, shown left. roof sheathing boards extend.

LEAN DECORATION

The scroll saw was a great contributor to decoration in these cottages with complex patterns emerging from repetitive shapes, but some of the most ornate facades evolved from the simple use of sticks of wood arranged into elaborate patterns. Often these sticks are as small as 1" square. These compositions of wood often function as ways to use light and shadow as essential to the experience.

Columns and posts could range from simple to complex, even lathe-turned in later years. When a simple post was used it is typically enhanced with decorative brackets. Some of the very complex designs for these turn up in multiple camps suggesting that these details could be ordered up for installation.

Left: Two column capitals, probably designed recently by an architect, but well within the tradition--Craigville, MA.
Above: "Snowbound "with elegant column trim. This design is also found in other campgrounds and may have been commercially available.
Below: Detail of brackets suggesting trees--from South Seaville cottage on cover of this book.

VERY LEAN COLUMNS

These columns reflect lean thinking in a Southern arbor or tabernacle. This structure has had a new slab installed, but the original simple foundation and tree-trunk post are set on something as common as a large stone, with a knick in the beam to seat a bracket.

Below: Two thin very thin pieces of wood, perhaps 1-1/2" x 3-1/2" surround a slim post and provide enough strength to support a porch in Indian Field Camp, near Georgetown, SC. Today this would have required a large beam or engineered lumber instead.

STRUCTURE AND FRAMING

Structures and framing were not standardized at this time. The skill and lore of carpenters led to experimentation and creativity. Structural engineering as we know it today evolved in the later years of the 19th century with the development of the skyscraper, and it was not widely available for the construction of Camp Meeting type buildings. What we find are unique details that sometimes worked well. A cottage in the Boulder, CO, Chautauqua is framed with the rafters parallel to the ridge. It is unclear what advantage this gave—perhaps it supported the cottages in the face of strong winds better. Porch framing in many Camps was an exercise in extemporization and expansion. As in any vernacular tradition, what started as crude framing often became quite sophisticated, especially when more money was available to solve problems of second story porches expanding over first floor porches, as seen in the example from Oak Bluffs, Martha's Vineyard. Some examples also show structural members that seem to be little more than matchsticks, though the quality of wood available at this time was far better than what is available today.

Sometimes buildings begin to lean. Sometimes this is due to insubstantial foundations, or sometimes it reflects pure neglect and rot. As mentioned earlier, it is common to see these buildings moved, which explains how close they end up, often touching. But, it is surprising to see tiny buildings with very small framing pieces survive extreme weather. Proof that this kind of building

Above left: Gently leaning cottage, Asbury Grove, could be pulled back to plumb with relative ease. The scale of repair is manageable.
Above right: Cottage resting on stacked concrete blocks showing strain at corner. Cottages were easy to move and foundations informal.
Below: rafters parallel to ridge, possibly a variant on post and beam framing. Right: Cottages at Camp Faithful, touching, undoubtedly moved.

Good example of porch framing as a progressive and expressive exercise, subject to expansion and revision. Lower right shows the same cottage a few years later, different colors but showing the adaptive nature of the porch as well as how a shed addition has been accommodated.

Left: A more sophisticated way to frame a porch. Note the integrated upper and lower porch where the dramatic brackets found on the porch act as structural supports for the second floor deck. The porch gets a roof that is part flat and part sloped.

This elegant cottage faces the tabernacle in Oak Bluffs, Martha's Vineyard, MA.

Right: Examples of minimal support brackets carrying a sleeping porch at the upper right and the front deck on the lower left. The front porch and deck show evidence that it used to incorporate a large tree that must have died and was removed.

Lower far right: Another view of the sleeping porch and a cottage that has been cut away to incorporate trees.

Above: a rare example of a completely new cottage built in the old way with the consent of the local building inspector. Hand cut oak columns and gothic window trim enlivened with some bright colors

The Sleeping Porch addition.
Below: trimmed roof to accommodate trees.

Note tree stump at lower left with porch adapted around it. At one point the porch would have incorporated the tree.

GABLES AND BALLOON FRAMING

With balloon framing and plate heights at 12' generally, sheathing a gable end offered another opportunity for decoration. Standard lumber lengths were not long enough to reach the entire height of the cottage so the upper level vertical siding frequently ran over the lower siding with opportunities for creative transitions. The cottage on the facing page uses wood that has been cut on a 45 degree angle to create vertical, beveled battens. In this case, the batten depth is nearly exactly the thickness of the vertical upper pieces making for a precise geometry. Bayside Camp Ground has a number of complex cottages that resolve their geometries well.

Above: close-up of a rake design made from small, scroll-saw cut incremental pieces.

Left: Cottage at Camp Etna, in poor condition, but showing a finely resolved gable design, terminating clapboards with vertical decorative siding.

This page: more complex geometry in Bay-side, ME, cottages and coordinated bracket

Right top and bottom: Some examples of pierced wood decoration in Ocean Grove, NJ, another decorative pattern found in many Camp Grounds. Ocean Grove has many large examples of this level of decoration.

Below: Association Cottage, Plainville, CT, an excellent example of using simple sticks for complex design. Bottom, left: highly decorated scroll-saw cut detailing, Wesleyan Grove Camp Meeting, Martha's Vineyard, MA.

Extremely fine grained surface detail is also found on Cottages. Above a well detailed cottage in Monteagle, TN, represents a pattern found there for angled front cottages with wrap-around porches. Below: shingle detail from Etna, ME.
Right: Paired roof brackets at Craigville, MA.
Opposite page, well detailed cottage, Bayside, ME, with detail of brackets and structural ties

Left: Cottage in Round Lake, NY with a number of popular details on one of the earlier cottages there.
Below: Two examples from Laurel Park, Northampton, MA that demonstrate a wood skeleton to the exterior of the vertical siding. As most Cottages are usually one thin layer of vertical siding attached to a timber frame, this is an innovation.

Right top: Simple detailing using plain cut wood to achieve decoration. Porch end wall is interesting with sandwiching boards and then splaying them. This cottage also demonstrates a simple column fabricated from smaller members wih a decorative spacing detail. Again, decoration and structure merged.

Below Right: Martha's Vineyard cottage showing a lathe turned balustrade. So called "pew style" balustrades are more common. The column brackets, atop turned columns are more sympathetic to that style, and it is unusual to find them blended.

Above: Very old cottages, Empire Camp Meeting, Poland, ME. This camp has moved cottages together into groups, perhaps to reduce fire threat, or to increase available size. This unusual roofing treatment seems to be a compromise for cost or availability of materials. Camp cats are common.

Below: a vernacular response to tiny cottage and need for a porch. When you are seated, a high ceiling isn't necessary and the roof line gets resolved easily.

Left above: Hedding Camp elegant cottage with another starburst detail and good formal lines.

Far left below: Willimantic cottage with simple, thin bent wood railing detail.

Left: Pew-style railing, the most typical form of baluster in New England Camp Meetings which allows for myriad design options.

Above: Wooden sidewalk along a street in Round Lake, NY.
Left: Old Cottages survive winter of 2015, Asbury Grove, Hamilton, MA.
Right top: Lean and simple rear exit from cottage near Skowhegan ME.
Right bottom: Wooden trestle walks connect Camp Ground across steep ravines at Monteagle.

CHAPTER 6 -- SOUTHERN CAMPS

If the traditional cottages of the northeast challenge our concept of "house" with their scale and detailing, the Southern Camp Grounds challenge our concepts of community by stripping away our thinking about what is necessary for an intense experience of community.

I went searching for Rock Springs Camp Meeting in Denver, Catawba County, NC, because it is the longest continuously operated Camp Meeting in the country. It dates from 1794 and it was the first Southern Camp I had seen. When I arrived on a rainy May day, pre-season, I was immediately stunned by the appearance of the place. It resembled something between a stockyard and a concentration camp. There were no windows, only slots in the rough, unpainted siding, concrete floors or dirt, metal roofs on leaning porch structures and grassy pathways. I couldn't imagine Americans in the 21st century inhabiting such a place, not to mention that they came every year. I determined to return in season, late July and early August.

In May, I also found Motts Grove Camp, nearby, which is an Afro-American camp established in 1850, clearly before the Civil War. Some of the early history of Camp Meetings suggests that slaves accompanied their masters and were housed in a different area of tents. (See the History section for a map indicating this). That land was given to slaves to establish Camp Meetings opens up another area of inquiry. I later found the locations of 2 more Afro-American Camp Meetings in South Carolina near Harleyville. I was able to locate St. Pauls' and Shady Grove Camps via Internet map search but didn't have time to go there. They are active and clearly

Off-season, a place like Rock Springs Camp is difficult to understand. Opposite hand, afternoon as the Camp has been set up for its Season. Below right: A view through porches at Mt. Pleasant, NC. Individual porches are private space. Promenade space is exterior to the porches.

isting, established in 1860—at the beginning of the Civil War.
they are extremely close to Indian Field, Cypress and not too far
om Cattle Creek Camp Meeting. Pursuing the history of black
amp Meetings is a worthy search; there is a great deal more to be
arned.

lso visited Balls Creek Camp, established 1853, in Catawba
y, NC. The layout of Balls Creek is very similar to the layout
Rock Springs and they are only about a half hour's drive apart.
lls Creek is brightly painted and provides a strong contrast with
ck Springs and Mott's Grove, though the form of the "tents"
d continuous circumferential paths is similar. I am told that the
ight colors are a more recent phenomenon. And as always, no
ndows, just slits—a concept that reminds us that ventilation,
ivacy and views are functions.

eturned in the hot and humid season of Rock Springs. It was in
e upper 90s with humidity that is tropical. I arrived in the early
ernoon and my first surprise was that each "tent" front had at
st one and sometimes several porch swings hanging from the
nt edge of the galvanized steel roofed porches. The plain wood
iches that are built along the back of the porch—at the face
the wood tent with its slotted openings--had colorful fabrics or
ilts hung against them. I was to learn this was partly decoration
t actually to prevent wood splinters for people sitting there.
hat had looked like livestock pens were now open and basic
chens and kitchen tables were visible along with refrigerators,
ves and sinks. People were setting up decorations, turning on
rhead fans or window fans. Large numbers of people were

visiting, setting up, or wandering. Children ran and played, the grass had been mowed.

It became evident that the slots were an adaptation to the event. A window was unnecessary—there was no better view than sitting on the porch. What was needed was privacy for the upstairs sleeping area and very much for ventilation. I saw the details that would have allowed the corrugated galvanized roofing to create convection currents to draw air into the slots and out, though I was unsure if I saw the exit vents at the roof. I do know that sitting under a tin roof in the heat of the day is an experience in infra-red heat, but some tents had started installing rigid insulation sheets at the porch ceilings and the difference was dramatic.

What was striking was the sense of community—even as a total stranger. I was invited in, talked to, welcome. The proximity of tent porch after tent porch with people simply sitting and visiting, formed the space, and following the people walking along the long promenade—reminded me of a *"ramblas"* experience. Being on that long promenade was an experience of being at once in private space—the distance between the tent porches, and public space by way of the long axis. This gives one the option to engage with people on porches or very comfortably keep walking.   Again, the voice level matched whether one was involved with private conversation or public interaction.

After a dinner break, I came back at full darkness, with heat like a damp blanket. I remember talking to a woman who had hurried to the camp after a long day of work to get organized for the event. An elderly woman who had been coming to camp since childhood showed me her tent including the area where she had created a first floor shower area that had only just enough privacy

so that the breeze was not shut off. I learned that when the camp was electrified, they only went with 20Amp service—not enough to allow for air conditioning. This guarantees that people are out and seeing others. I saw the "history" tent which is a very old "first tent" made from hand-hewn, squared off stacked logs and a straw floor. When they have rebuilt tents, the form is very much the same but with the addition of pressure-treated lumber and concrete floors.

As night came on, services began at the central "Arbor" or tabernacle. Sitting in the first row of "tents" it was possible to monitor what was going, but noise from within the tent did not carry back to the Arbor and children could play. The Tents are through units. One side on the inner square is formal and the back is the communal promenade. Rock Springs is large enough that parts of a second and third ring are also well-used there. The social activity on the outer rings gets even more informal with little ball games happening between grownups and children. Generations come together; I never heard a child cry. People inherently understood the concept of how loud to make a voice to carry the distance either across the approximate 30' wide separation or lower to limit conservation to the porch or inside the house. Privacy was also a product of behavior in community.

As it gets darker, the slot openings on the tents begin to glow like a series of lanterns creating the right level of light and darkness that allows conversation, privacy, participation by choice. The preaching at the center was well attended but far more people were on the back pathways of the Camp. I wondered if it was still about revival, and at the end of the service I heard a big bell being rung. Curious as to what this was, I went into the center area to find that they lift the smaller children up so they can experience ringing th

Night shots of Rock Springs Camp Ground showing promenade and lantern effect by night. Opposite: Afternoon at Rock Springs and walkers at Balls Creek below right.

ell. There are a lot of reasons while children love Camp Meetings.

What is hard to describe is the satisfaction, even as a stranger, f being in this intense experience of community. The complete romenade on the back side of the cottages is close to a half mile round and carries many people. Part of why people come back nnually by the thousands (I estimate many thousands that night) o these places is that, in the current 21st century American world, ve yearn for this direct experience of ourselves as a society and a ulture. Community is possible in the leanest of conditions, and erhaps better because of it.

STUDYING THE SOUTHERN CAMPGROUND

urprisingly, when I have measured southern 'tents', I find they re very close to 12'-4" wide putting them into the same size nge as the older northeast camps. It may have been based on anvas tents and the dimensions recommended by Circuit Riders. hese itinerant ministers also influenced the Methodist Camp Meetings toward standardization. The original intention was to eate the kind of space that could generate Revival, and they had serve that purpose; but even the Circuit Riders understood the nportance of the dual value to create a community that would rry the message forward. The need to separate from daily life

generated the need to create a sense of enclosure for the Camp. The focus was on the central area for the preaching; the necessary support areas were also important to the Camp Meeting's success.

The effect of a place like Indian Field is stunning—a full circle of nearly identical, linked structures facing the center. Particularly after coming through some of the narrow passages between kitchen and side space, the effect can be breathtaking; the transformation of mind--instantaneous. That the tents at Indian Fields resemble Carolina tobacco barns becomes irrelevant. You have a sense of what holy ground should be. It's certain that the functional experience doesn't remain that formal; the wide green apron between the tents and the tabernacle will be used by children and people sitting on blankets, but the first impression is singular.

The two dogtrot camps I visited, Old Lebanon and South Union, MS, present another complex form that organized space into public, private and intimate. The central "trot" in a hot time offers shade, breeze and visiting. The rear side, like any camp meeting is the informal side with cooking and dining. The sleeping space is in the enclosed areas. At Old Lebanon there was an example of a 3 way dog-trot. In which a third covered space extended to a third wing of a cottage.

Details are understated and undeniably lean. A header carrying a porch roof is made up of a flat 2x4 plate and a vertical 2 x 4 set around a thin wood post. One piece reinforces the next. Benches seem to provide lateral support for the uprights. The interiors are simple. These places are wide open out of season making one reassess the concept of owning "stuff". The places are not completely empty; there are big tables, some sleep platforms, simpl counters, benches, the odd salvaged sink with a single water spigot, and usually a brick or concrete block barbecue set-up.

The walls of the old tents darken naturally, grow various kinds of mold, get repairs and changes, becoming a palimpsest of past and present. The spaces between things become important, the exterior radius of kitchens at Cattle Creek and Indian Fields offer a shifting perspective connecting people on the informal side. Sometimes a view yields a symphony of individual stovepipes, or suggests enormous barbecue potential.

Sometimes there is a chapel and many Southern Camps have attached cemeteries so that homecoming also suggests a communit uninterrupted, that spans generations.

Above: Cypress Creek Methodist Camp

Lean Kitchen

Protected Kitchens - Indian Field Camp

Above and left: Tent details at Cattle Creek Camp, "possessionlees space"
Below: Panorama of Indian Field Camp, near St. George, SC

Park Drive - rear view, Bayside, ME,

*Craigville, MA, cottage undergoing intense restoration. Some historic detail
is visible including vertical siding which has been covered over with shingles.*

COTTAGE COMMUNITIES - THE AMERICAN CAMP MEETING MOVEMENT
A Study in Lean Urbanism

CAMP MEETING MASTER LIST researched for *this* book. There are estimated to be about 1000 remaining Camp Grounds still in existence in varying states of preservation.

Alton Bay Camp Meeting Ground, Alton Bay, NH 1863

Asbury Grove Camp Meeting Association, Hamilton, MA 1863

Balls Creek Camp Ground, Maiden, Catawba NC (Methodist) 1856

Bayside, Northport, ME (platted) 1849 (1873?)

Beershiba Springs, ME, TN circa 1952

Boulder Chautaqua, Boulder CO 1898

Camp Greene, Greene, RI, Adventist Christian Church 1871

Camp Woods, Ossining, NY 1804

Cattle Creek Camp Meeting ground, Branchville, SC 1786

Craigville Camp, Centerville, MA 1872

Cypress Methodist Camp, Ridgeville, SC, 1801

Chautauqua, NY. The Chautauqua Institution, 1874

Douglas Camp, Douglas, MA 1875 (Adventist)

Empire Grove Camp, E. Poland, ME 1834

Etna Camp, Etna, ME (Independent Spiritualist) 1876

Framingham Chautauqua, Framingham, MA 1872,1880

Greene, RI, Camp Greene, (Adventist), 1870

Haddam, CT, Camp Bethel (Adventist) 1878

Hedding Camp Meeting Association. Epping, NH 1863

Indian Field Camp Meeting, St. George, SC 1794

Inglebrook Camp, Gatlinburg, TN –approx 1870

Lake Pleasant Camp Meeting Association 1879, near Montague, MA (Spiritualist)

Lakeside Camp Meeting, Belgrade, ME (Advent Christian Church)

Laurel Park, Northampton, MA (condo) 1872

Lily Dale, Lily Dale, NY (Spiritualist, 1879

Madison Spiritualist Camp, near Skowhegan, ME

Malaga Camp, Newfield, NJ 1869

Marion, MA, T.A.C.C.A. Camp, ca. 1890 (Adventist)

Matha's Vineyard Camp Meeting Associations, Oak Bluffs, MA 1835

Monteagle Assembly, Monteagle, TN 1882

Potts Grove Campground, near Terrell, NC 1872, 1850

Mt. Tabor, Parsippany, NJ, 1869 (platted as town)

Neshoba County Fairgrounds, Philadelpia, MS 1889 (private fairground)

Niantic, CT, Pine Grove Camp Meeting Association. (Spiritualist)

Ocean Park, Old Orchard Beach, ME, Oceanwood (Baptist), 1881

Ocean Grove, Neptune, NJ 1869

Old Orchard Beach, Camp ME . (Salvation Army), 1870

Old Lebanon Camp, Ackerman, MS 1840

Pine Grove, *New England 1867

Pitman Grove, Pitman, NJ, 1871 (platted as town now)

Plainville, Camp Grounds Association, Plainville, CT 1865

Pleasant Grove Camp, Mineral Springs, NC 1850 (Methodist) 1787

Portsmouth, RI Camp Meeting Ground, Portsmouth, RI 1890

Rock Springs Camp Meeting, Denver, NC, 1794, (Methodist)

Round Lake Village, Malta Township, NY 1867,1868

South Union Camp Meeting, near Ackerman, MS 1865

South Seaville Camp Meeting, South Seaville, NJ (Sea Isle), (Methodist) 1863

Southington, CT Camp Faithful (Adventist), 1869

Sterling Camp, Sterling MA (now Waushacum Village Homeowner's Assn.),1852

Temple Heights, Northport, ME, (Spiritualist), 1883

Willimantic Camp Meeting Grounds, Willimantic, CT (Methodist),1860

Winnipesaukee Camp, Laconia, NH 1868

Yarmouth Camp Meeting, Yarmouth, MA 1819

* People who own properties in Camp Meeting Grounds often want to keep the privacy, peace and quiet of the place and in respect of their wishes, this camp ground is not further located.

BIBLIOGRAPHY

Bayside Historical Preservation Society, *If These Cottages Could Talk* - *a history of Bayside, Northport, Maine,* 2007. Contact P.O. Box 304, Belfast, Maine, 04915

Bishir, Catherine W. and graphics, Lounsbury, Carl, *North Carolina Architecture* , The Historic Preservation Society of North Carolina, 1990.

Brown, Dr. Kenneth O., Ph.d. *Holy Ground Too, The Camp Meeting Family Tree.* Hazleton, Pennsylvania, Holiness Archives, copyright 1997 by Kenneth O. Brown, 243 S. Pine St., Hazleton, PA 18201

Craycroft, Robert, *The Neshoba County, Fair, Place and Paradox in Mississippi,* Center for Small Town Research and Design, Mississippi State University, University – Capital Press of Mississippi, Jackson, MS, 1989

DuBois, Charles, L. *Malaga Camp Recollections.* Brochure, 1994.

FitzGerald, Frances. *Cities on a Hill, New York,* Simon and Shuster, 1986.

Gorham, B. Weed, *The Camp Meeting Manual, A Practical Book for the Camp Ground,* Boston, H.V. Degen, Boston, 1854

Hayden, Dolores, *Seven American Utopias, The Architecture of Communitarian Socialism (1790-1975).* Cambridge, MIT Press, 1976.

Massabeau, W.A., *The Camp Meeting in South Carolina Methodism,* talk delivered 11/4/1919 by permission of Wofford College. Wofford College,, Digital Commons Collection

Pope, Arthur, K. *The Heart Strangely Warmed, The Chautauqua and Methodist Campgrounds at Plainville, Connecticut.,* Trafford Publishing, 2006.

Robertson, James A. *Hedding Among the Pines. A History of Hedding Camp Meeting Grounds, Epping, New Hampshire,* Publishing Works, Epping, NH. 2008

Turner, John G., *Brigham Young: Pioneer Prophet,* Belknap Press, 2014

Weiss, Ellen. *City in the Woods, The Life and Design of an American Camp Meeting on Martha's Vineyard.* New York, Oxford University Press, 1987, Boston, Northeastern University Press, 1998

Wicker, Christine, *Lily Dale, the True Story of the Town that Talks to the Dead,* Harper Collins, San Francisco, 2003.

http://www.centerforneweconomics.org/content/community-land-trusts-1 a website that studies land trusts today and how they can be utilized.

Above: Asbury Grove in disastrous 2015 winter. Both these cottages survived with no damage. See page 57 to see these two in summer.
Right: High Pines shelter a Camp Meeting Circle, Pine Grove, and below, the sand streets of South Seaville Camp, NJ.

Above: Alton Bay Camp Meeting, Alton, NH, in 2008. In 2009 a wind driven fire burned 53 cottages in one hour. These cottages, so close that they were reached only by footpath, were all destroyed. Preservation of these very special places as well as the ability to rebuild is alwasys an essential concern.

About the author

Sara N. Hines is an architect and urban designer. She has practiced architecture in many states and is currently based in Massachusetts where she continues to visit and study Cottage Communities and Camp Meetings. She is interested in the preservation of these wonderful places and the heritage that they embody. Email: infoCottageCommunities@gmail.com.

Made in the USA
San Bernardino, CA
29 July 2016